THE DUTCH IN AMERICA

The IN AMERICA *Series*

THE **DUTCH** IN AMERICA

GERRIT J. TENZYTHOFF, Ph.D.

Director
Religious Studies Department
Southwest Missouri State College

Published by
Lerner Publications Company
Minneapolis, Minnesota

ACKNOWLEDGMENTS

The illustrations are reproduced through the courtesy of: pp. 6, 14, 32, 33, Library of Congress; pp. 7, 8, 10, 22, 29, 30, 34 (top and bottom), 41, 42, 44 (top and bottom), 47 (top and bottom), 48, 50, 52, 84, Netherlands Information Service; pp. 9, 11 (top left and bottom), 26, 27, 28, 31, 35, 72, 75, 83, 85, 88 (left), 90, 92, 93 (top left and top right), 97, 98 (top left, top right, and bottom), Independent Picture Service; p. 11 (top right), Mauritshuis, The Hague; pp. 12, 13, 39, 55, 59, Rijksmuseum, Amsterdam; pp. 15, 16, 23 (bottom), Museum of the City of New York; pp. 18, 49 (left and right), 57, 91, 94, *Dictionary of American Portraits*, Dover Publications, Inc; pp. 20, 21, Post Office Department, Division of Philately; p. 23 (top), Title Guarantee Company; p. 25, Municipal Museum, The Hague; pp. 36, 86, 87, Rutgers University; p. 37 (left and right), Martinus Nijhoff N.V.; p. 40, *Mennonite Encyclopedia*; pp. 61, 77, Netherlands Information Bureau; p. 62 (top and bottom), State Historical Society of Wisconsin; p. 64, Rijksvoorlichting Dienst; pp. 66, 67, 68, 69, 70, 80, Netherlands Museum, Holland, Michigan; p. 71 (top and bottom), Pella Chamber of Commerce; pp. 74, 93 (bottom left), Michigan Historical Commission; p. 78, Wells Fargo Bank History Room; p. 81, Northwestern College, Orange City, Iowa; p. 88 (right), Columbia University; p. 89 (left), Pearl S. Buck, p. 89 (right), Little, Brown and Company; p. 93 (bottom right), Office of the Mayor; p. 95 (top left and top right), Defense Department; p. 95 (bottom left and bottom right), Massachusetts Institute of Technology; p. 96 (left), University of Utah Medical Center; p. 96 (right), University of Iowa; p. 99 (top left), Minnesota Vikings; p. 99 (top right), Baseball Hall of Fame; p. 99 (bottom left), Minnesota Twins; p. 99 (bottom right), United Press International; p. 100, Windmill Island Municipal Park.

The Library of Congress Cataloged the
original printing of this title as follows:

TenZythoff, Gerrit J.
    The Dutch in America [by] Gerrit J. tenZythoff. Minneapolis,
Minn., Lerner Publications Co. [1969]

    104 p. illus., facsim., maps, ports. 24 cm. (The In America
series)

    The history of the Dutch in the New World from 1664 to the
present describing their contributions to their adopted homeland and culture as farmers, traders, fighters, and artists.

    1. Dutch in the United States—Juvenile literature. [1. Dutch
in the United States] I. Title.

E184.D9T4   301.453′492′073   68-31505
ISBN 0-8225-0220-8 [Library]
ISBN 0-8225-1005-7 [Paper]

International Standard Book Number: 0-8225-0220-8 Library Edition
International Standard Book Number: 0-8225-1005-7 Paper Edition

Library of Congress Catalog Card Number: 68-31505

Fourth Printing 1976

...CONTENTS...

Dutch traders. Early merchants in New Netherland were impressed with the rich supply of furs that could be found there. In 1621, the Dutch government encouraged the traders to band together and form the West India Company rather than continue to compete separately.

The Hague, South Holland. Parliament buildings surround the Hall of Knights, a former hunting lodge built by the Counts of Holland in the thirteenth century. The surrounding gardens, called the "s-Gravenhage" or "gardens of the Count," gave the city its name.

Introduction

It is not surprising that two such different names as "Holland" and "The Netherlands" refer to the same country. Originally, Holland was the richest and most prominent of the seven provinces which formed the Republic of the United Netherlands. Until the end of the eighteenth century, Holland usually dominated and controlled the other provinces to such an extent that The Netherlands, as a whole, was often called "Holland." Then in 1795, the Republic was captured by the French and remained under their rule until 1813, when Napoleon was defeated. In 1815, the country was reinstated as the Kingdom of The Netherlands ruled by the House of Orange-Nassau as hereditary monarchs, but the custom of calling the country "Holland" continued.

The Kingdom of The Netherlands now includes 11 provinces of which the original province of Holland became two: North Holland and South Holland. Amsterdam, in North Holland, is the country's capital because it is the official residence of the ruling House of Orange. The Hague, in South Holland, is the seat of the elected national government. In this book we use "Holland" to refer to the two provinces of North and South Holland. We use "The Netherlands" to refer to the country as a whole.

The word "Dutch" also refers to The Netherlands. The English probably borrowed the word from the German word *Deutsch*. Dutch and *Deutsch* sound much the same, but today "Dutch" refers to The Netherlands and *Deutsch* means "German" in its English translation.

Frequently, the Dutch are confused with the Pennsylvania Dutch, who are really Pennsylvania *Deutsch* (or German) rather than Dutch. Even though many of their ancestors lived in The Netherlands, the Pennsylvania Dutch were in Germany for such a long time before coming to the United States that they adopted German as their language. For that reason the Pennsylvania Dutch are unable to understand the language of The Netherlands Dutch.

Dutch women of Scheveningen, Holland, work to repair the fishing nets. They wear the dress of their village. Wooden shoes keep their feet drier than would leather shoes.

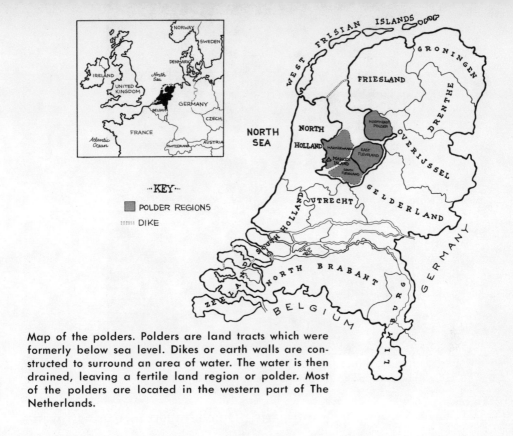

Map of the polders. Polders are land tracts which were formerly below sea level. Dikes or earth walls are constructed to surround an area of water. The water is then drained, leaving a fertile land region or polder. Most of the polders are located in the western part of The Netherlands.

PART I

The Dutch in the New World

1. *Farmers and Traders*

The Dutch say: "God created the world, but we made our land." How did they make it? They built (and are still building) dikes, huge dams that keep the ocean out. Behind the dikes lay fertile soil, deposited over thousands of years by the rivers Rhine, Meuse, and Scheldt. On this land below the sea, farmers began to use windmills to keep the ever-rising water at the most desirable level. They learned to grow luscious crops of vegetables. On the grass lands, their cows produced milk of such a consistently high grade that Dutch cheese became a symbol of quality.

Dike construction. Dikes prevent water from flooding back onto the polders or reclaimed land areas.

As agriculture brought prosperity, Dutch traders increasingly used the rivers for their journeys. They could travel easily through most of Europe. Across the North Sea they went to England and on the Baltic Sea they reached Scandinavia and Russia. The Netherlands thus became a nation of farmers and traders.

2. The New World

Columbus's discovery of a new world in 1492 created a stir among the traders in Europe. They began to seek a new, safer passage to the lands of the Far East by way of America. The overland trade routes were long, dangerous, and expensive.

In 1492, The Netherlands was not yet an independent nation. It was part of the larger Burgundian empire. In 1506, Charles, the young grandson of the Spanish rulers Ferdinand and Isabella, inherited the Burgundian lands of his father; when Ferdinand died he also inherited Spain. One man, thus, held both Spain and The Netherlands. In 1519, Charles became Holy Roman Emperor. Known as Charles V, he ruled over territory stretching from Austria to The Lowlands and Spain.

King **Philip II** of Spain (1527-1598) and **William the Silent** of The Netherlands (1533-1584). When Philip's policy of dictatorship met resistance, he brought the Spanish Inquisition to Holland. William, who had served under Philip, was so enraged by this action that he broke from Philip and afterwards worked to expel the Spanish from The Netherlands.

Shortly before his death in 1558, he gave The Netherlands and Spain to his son Philip II (1527-1598) of Spain. Philip disregarded and violated the religious and political freedom of the Netherlanders to such an extent that the Dutch revolted in defense of their traditional rights. It took 80 years of war with Spain, from 1568 until 1648, before The Netherlands succeeded in gaining recognition as an independent state.

King Philip II parts in anger from William the Silent. The northern provinces, under the leadership of William, succeeded in forcing the Spanish armies to leave. Philip labeled William a traitor and put a high price on his head in 1581. William was assassinated at Delft in 1584.

Taking the oath on the Peace Treaty of Westphalia, 1648. The treaty granted independence for The Netherlands and declared a policy of greater religious toleration.

Long before The Netherlands and Spain signed the Peace Treaty of Westphalia in 1648, the Dutch had created a navy that carried the war against Spain into both East and West Indies. Without the fishermen's contribution of men and ships, however, there would not have been a Dutch navy. Their new sea power enabled the Dutch to gain control of overseas territories from Spain, thus creating a colonial empire that made it possible for Dutch merchants to compete for commercial leadership in Europe.

To reach the East Indies, Dutch ships had to take the long route past the Spanish peninsula and around the Cape of Good Hope. Inevitable war losses in lives and ships caused the merchants to look for safer and shorter routes. For instance, as early as 1584, the energetic trader Balthasar de Moucheron proposed that his trading post at Archangel, the Muscovite port on the Arctic Sea, be used as the base from which to search for a Northeast Passage around Russia and Siberia to the East Indies. His townsman Willem Usselincx disagreed. Instead of avoiding the Spanish enemy, he argued, The Netherlands should establish colonies in the New World. These settlements could serve as bases to carry the war against Spain right into her colonies, the source of her wealth.

Willem Usselincx of Middelburg wanted The Netherlands to colonize the New World.

The Netherlands' government certainly wanted to encourage trade with the East Indies. In 1602 it chartered the United East India Company for just that purpose. But Usselincx' plan for colonization did not gain approval. It seemed too big an undertaking for a small country, especially since The Netherlands was in desperate need of more people and a stronger economy. Dutch farmers wanted to recover more land from the sea rather than to establish plantations beyond the sea.

However, De Moucheron's proposal to find a Northeast Passage to the East Indies promised the quick profits that were so urgently needed to finance the war. The government encouraged the United East India Company to attempt a trial sailing around Russia to the Far East. The Company engaged an English skipper named Henry Hudson to find the Northeast Passage.

On April 6, 1609, Henry Hudson began his journey on the *Halve Maen* (Half Moon). Once he had gone north, he turned to the west and not to the east. Since no one had sailed the Arctic before, it is possible that his maps were not accurate. But it is more likely that Hudson had heard fishermen's tales about an unexplored river that might provide the long-sought passage leading to the East Indies through America.

Vague word had spread about Dutch whaling captains, operating in the Arctic Sea, who had occasionally been unable to return in time and had traveled southwest. They had used what is now Long Island to escape the fierce Arctic winter.

Henry Hudson violated his contract in the hope that his westward search might succeed and gain the belated approval of the United East India Company. By the first of July 1609, Hudson had come as

Henry Hudson abandoned. After his expedition for the Dutch, Hudson made a trip for the English in 1610. This time his crew mutinied and set him adrift.

far as Newfoundland. It took two additional months before he sighted Sandy Hook. On September 3, he dropped anchor in the mouth of what is now called the Hudson River. The fishermen had been right: there was a river. But the river did not provide access to the Indies and Cathay or China. When the *Halve Maen* had reached what is now Albany, the water was still fresh instead of somewhat salty. Hudson concluded that the sea on which China bordered could not be near at all. Captain and crew had failed in their mission to find the mysterious passage to the Far East.

Of course, Hudson had to return. Unwilling to face the Company, he stepped off the boat in England. In November, the rest of the crew took the *Halve Maen* back to The Netherlands where they gave a glowing report about the river and the possibilities to barter with the Indians. Some enterprising merchants did not wait for encouragement from the Company or the government. They simply crossed the Atlantic to go after the fur trade with the Indians. The French had thus far successfully monopolized that trade in their Nova Francia, or Canada. The British operated in Virginia. Between the holdings of those two giants a virgin territory lay open.

Usselincx' project to plant colonies in the New World was revived. But very few Dutchmen wanted to leave their homeland at this time. The Dutch economy could easily support the population. Social conditions were among the best in Europe. Many refugees, such as Jews expelled from Spain and Portugal, Puritans from England, and Huguenots from France, found religious and political toleration in The

Netherlands. Why should anyone want to leave a country that knew neither persecution nor poverty?

The merchants knew that they must act quickly to reap profits in the Hudson valley, for other countries were ready to step in. By the spring of 1613, skipper Adriaen Block arrived on his ship *Fortuyn* (Fortune). (Block Island, northeast of Long Island, is named after him.) Soon he saw his quiet trading with the Indians interrupted by skipper Thys Mossel who had sailed his square-sterned *Jonge Tobias* (Young Tobias) from Amsterdam to the Hudson. He offered the Indians twice the amount that Block paid for beaver skins. At last, with great difficulty, the two skippers came to a degree of understanding. However, when summer came and it was time to return to The Netherlands, Block and Mossel were so afraid of losing their Indian suppliers that

Adriaen Block's map of New Netherland, 1614. It was the first map to bear the name "New Netherland" and was presented to The Netherlands Estates-General by 13 businessmen.

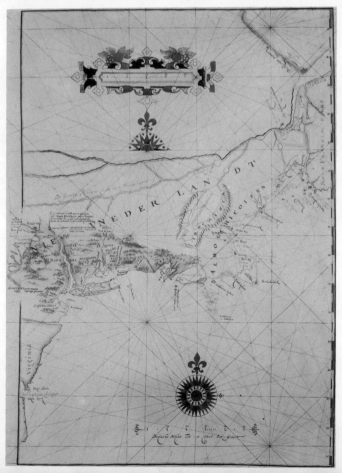

Timbers from Adriaen Block's ship, *Tiger.* It was burned during the winter of 1613-1614.

each left parties behind to continue trading. Thus Block's sponsor, the Van Tweenhuysen Company, became the owner of the first Dutch "settlement": Fort Nassau, on Castle Island in the Hudson River near Albany.

Since permanent trading posts had become necessary, the sponsoring Dutch companies decided that their ships should spend the winter of 1613-1614 on the Hudson River. It was then that skipper Block's ship *Tijger* (Tiger) caught fire. Was the fire set intentionally? The competing firms denied it. But the incident made the Van Tweenhuysen Company realize the necessity of uniting firms that had a common interest. Also, the Dutch government began to take a greater interest in the Hudson area.

On March 27, 1614, the government stated the requirements of trade in New Netherland, a territory between the 40th and the 45th parallels that seemed to belong to neither France nor England. Only those companies that had sailed to the Hudson River in 1614 could apply for a patent to make four voyages which were to be completed within three years. This gave the competing merchants an incentive to overcome their differences. By banding together, they could monopolize the profitable fur trade. Thus, in October of 1614, the New Netherland Company—comprised of these Dutch trading companies—received official permission to operate.

Competition did not, however, come to an end. New Netherland was a vast area. Who could prove that a Dutch applicant had not been there? The New Netherland Company was unable to stifle the merchants who had been excluded from the new company and wanted their share in a profitable market. The Dutch government hesitated to grant exclusive rights to the New Netherland Company, for this would mean that the American extension of the Dutch Republic would be the exclusive territory of a few merchants. Six of the United Provinces would surely protest if merchants from the seventh province, Holland, were to receive such advantages. Therefore, the government granted additional patents to other merchants in spite of the appeals of the New Netherland Company.

The Indians benefited from the competition. They became selective bargainers as so many merchants presented their wares. Not satisfied with kettles, axes, knives, and beads, they would try to come aboard the Dutch ships to see for themselves what they might like. Hendrik Christiaensen, skipper of the *Zwarte Beer* (Black Bear), and most of his crew were killed in a fight resulting from one such incident.

3. *West India Company*

The New Netherland Company did not succeed in renewing its charter, although it continued its activities for a time. The Dutch government wanted to end the policy of granting trade privileges to competing companies. Trade had certainly resulted in profits, but it caused too much confusion in New Netherland. The Dutch national interest could not be left in the hands of competing merchants. Usselincx' old plan to establish colonies in the New World gained favorable attention at last.

Slowly the government began to act. Early in 1620 the Van Tweenhuysen Company requested two Navy ships to protect a convoy that was to carry 400 families from The Netherlands and England to New Netherland. The government denied the request only because this was no time to antagonize either England or France, the giant neighbors to the south and north of the Dutch stake in America. The truce with Spain was about to end. Should war with Spain be resumed, The Netherlands needed good relations with France and England even more than bases in America.

In 1621, war with Spain broke out again. Now, however, the Dutch government decided to take advantage of the opportunities that New Netherland offered even at the risk of antagonizing England and

France. On June 3, 1621, the government induced the merchants to create a West India Company that was to have vast powers in New Netherland and additional territories that might be conquered. The Company was given the right to make treaties with the natives and to exercise every governmental power, including the right to declare war. Naturally, the Company was allowed to plant colonies where necessary. After 30 years, Usselincx' campaign for settlements in the New World was finally beginning to take hold.

Merchant **Kiliaen van Rensselaer** (1585-1644) helped found the West India Company. He later became one of its first patroons.

The task assigned to the West India Company was by no means limited to New Netherland. Its 24-year charter covered territories on both coasts of North and South America. Even Australia and all territories between the Cape of Good Hope and the eastern part of New Guinea were included. The Company's involvement in New Netherland was merely a fragment of its huge task. Each province of the United Republic assumed responsibility for a specific area under the Company's control. For instance, the province of Zeeland developed particular interest in South America, while the province of Holland, and especially Amsterdam, assumed responsibility for North America and New Netherland. One of the Company's first directors in Amsterdam, the jeweler Kiliaen van Rensselaer, became very prominent in New Netherland's affairs.

Although The Netherlands lacked the strength to completely subdue Spain, it could use the West India Company to attempt permanent settlements in territories taken away from Spain. The islands today referred to as the Dutch West Indies (the islands of Curaçao, Bonaire, Aruba, etc.) were annexed at that time.

The Company's charter specified that its territory extended north as far as Cape Race on New Foundland. And while the war was mainly fought in Spanish territories farther south, the Company soon tried to strengthen existing settlements in the Hudson River area, especially the small fort on Nut Island just off Manhattan, now known as Governor's Island. Fortifications were built on the Connecticut and Delaware Rivers. But for any chance of victory, these forts had to be converted into more permanent settlements.

In New Netherland, the Company had to choose between Fort Nassau and Manhattan Island as the best place for its boundary. Fort Nassau, near Albany, had the advantage of being far inland, making a surprise attack by the Spaniards impossible. For that reason, it gained initial favor.

4. *The Walloons*

In May 1624, skipper Cornelis Jacob May brought the first group of permanent settlers to New Netherland. The group consisted of 30 Walloon families and a number of single men. At least 18 of the families were directed to Castle Island, where Fort Nassau had stood until it was destroyed by an overflow of the Hudson River in 1617. Soon they moved from Castle Island to the west shore of the Hudson where they established Fort Orange, later called Albany. Meanwhile, the Company had directed two families and eight single men to the Fresh River, now the Connecticut River. Two more families and six single men were settled on what is now the Delaware River. Only eight

In 1924, the United States Government issued a stamp to commemorate the coming of the Walloons to New Netherland in 1624. It pictures the ship on which the settlers sailed.

single men were left for Manhattan Island. The small band of permanent settlers was spread so thin that within three years most of them were brought together again in the more advantageous concentration at New Amsterdam, which served as the Company's town and headquarters on Manhattan Island. The colony readily attracted the adventurous traders who came for quick profits, but these were few in number compared to the population of The Netherlands.

The 30 Walloon families were not native Dutchmen. Some of them were Huguenots (French Protestants) who had found refuge in The Netherlands after fleeing Cardinal Richelieu's France early in the seventeenth century. Others were descendants of French-speaking Protestants who had fled the Spanish Netherlands in the sixteenth century and had found safety from persecution in the Dutch Republic. The Dutch Reformed Church, with the aid of the national Dutch government, had created a string of French-speaking congregations for this early flock of refugees. These congregations were attached to the Reformed Church and were commonly known as the Walloon Church. The Walloons who arrived in New Netherland in 1624 were primarily French rather than Belgian. Without deep roots in The Netherlands, they were more inclined to look elsewhere for a permanent home.

It was true that the Dutch Republic had granted an exclusive position to the Reformed Church. In the life-and-death struggle with Spain, the religious issue was of great importance. Nevertheless, the

Seven United Provinces managed to work out compromises that made persecution of Roman Catholics extremely rare. The policies of the West India Company reflected a similar spirit of tolerance. The Provisional Order of 1623 had demanded that the Reformed Church be given an exclusive place in the Company's territories, but it also granted a large degree of freedom to other religions. Article Two of the Provisional Order reads:

> No other persons are allowed to practice religion within her territory [namely New Netherland] than those who adhere to the true, Reformed religion in the manner in which it is now being practiced in this country and who will thus by their Christian word and deed draw the Indians and other blind persons to the knowledge of God and his Word; without, however, persecuting any one on account of his religion, but permitting everyone liberty of conscience; however, should any one within her [the Company's] territory on purpose blaspheme the name of God and of our Savior Jesus Christ, he will be punished by the commander, or governor, and his council when such occasion arises.

Religious tolerance was not New Netherland's only attraction. Settlers were encouraged to come when they received enthusiastic letters from the first Walloons. The Company had invested free transportation for the colonists and would continue to do so for additional immigrants. In return, the settlers had to stay in the colony for a minimum of six years and had to raise specified crops. On the other hand, no colonist could be pressured into additional services without proper payment. Hence the settlers were known as "free colonists" in contrast to the indentured servants brought over by the Company. With the free colonists, the Company shared livestock and equipment on an equal basis.

This United States stamp of 1924 commemorates the landing of the Walloons in New Netherland, 1624.

But the Company did not want to risk becoming dependent upon the free colonists for its food supplies. Until 1652, the Company owned and operated its own farms as a supplement to the farming done by the free colonists. Indentured servants were brought over to operate these farms, although the Company attracted supervising head farmers by offering them equal share in cattle and crops. In 1625, the Company brought over five head farmers to supervise the first Company farms or *bouwerijen*.

It was also in 1625 that the Dutch surveyor, Krijn Frederiksz, staked out fortifications for the city of New Amsterdam that indentured servants were to build. In terms of the war against Spain, the Company had decided to strengthen Manhattan rather than the inland Fort Orange on the Hudson. If the Company were to ignore and neglect Manhattan, the enemy could conceivably seize it and bottle up the inland forts in spite of all their strength.

In 1626, Peter Minuit, a Huguenot, and governor of New Netherland, completed the purchase of Manhattan Island from the Indians for about $24 worth of trinkets. By the end of 1626, 30 houses had been built by simply digging a hole in the ground six or seven feet deep, lining the sides, floor, and roof with boards and bark, and adding needed partitions. A family might live for four years or more in such a "house" before moving into a more permanent home. (It is interesting that 200 years later, the Dutch settlers arriving in Iowa and Michigan used much the same kind of housing.)

Plan for New Amsterdam, 1625. "As soon as the moat will be complete, Commissioner Verhulst and the Council will immediately undertake the building of fortifications following concept (or plan) number C, which will be called Amsterdam, and will hire for digging as many hands as can be spared from among the construction workers, sailors, and colonists."

Peter Minuit purchases Manhattan Island, 1626. Minuit made New Amsterdam the center of the settlement.

5. *The Patroons*

In 1629, the commissioners for New Netherland, under the leadership of Kiliaen van Rensselaer, organized a campaign for a method that would enable the Company to populate the colony more quickly. The campaign resulted in the *Charter of Freedoms and Exemptions* which specified that the Company could grant a *patroonschap* (land plus ownership rights) to any members who wished to become *patroons* (land owners) by settling 50 people on their land within four years after registering their patroonschap with the Company.

Dutch settlers lay cobbles on the streets of New Amsterdam. (*Detail from diorama at the Museum of the City of New York*)

The *patroonschappen,* or land grants, in New Netherland were to be made on navigable rivers, either 12 miles along one bank or six miles along both banks. No limits were placed on the territory a patroon wished to claim going inland from the riverbank. Manhattan, however, remained the exclusive territory of the Company.

The patroons had unrestricted ownership of their lands and exercised full jurisdiction over their settlers. The patroons were given the rights to fish, hunt, farm, mill the grains, and trade. Only the fur trade was reserved for the Company.

A patroon's heir would automatically inherit the land as well as these rights. In other words, the outdated feudalistic order that had almost vanished in The Netherlands was now established in its colony. That fact alone doomed this land grant system to failure. Besides, the great powers entrusted to the patroons would almost inevitably clash with the rights of the Company. Even the governor of New Netherland lacked the jurisdiction that could force the patroons to act in the best interest of the colony as a whole.

The Company hoped, of course, that the patroon would develop his area by attracting farmers and artisans from The Netherlands and by building up good trade relations with the Indians. In each prospering patroonschap, the Company envisioned its own key port surrounded by fortifications for emergencies. The soldiers to be stationed in such forts could be more easily fed. Steady trading would strengthen and solidify New Netherland. The weakness of this plan lay in the patroons who readily assumed a large degree of independence. Not only did they quarrel among themselves, but they often defied the Company.

Of the five patroonships originally registered, only Rensselaerswijk (near Greenbush, New York) succeeded. While the Company had bought back the other four by 1635, Kiliaen van Rensselaer's patroonship met with moderate success and survived both the English occupation of New Netherland and the American Revolution. The heirs of Van Rensselaer did not give up their political rights until 1786. However, it wasn't until the Tin Horn Rebellion of 1844 that the tenants were freed from their service to the Van Rensselaer patroonship.

View of The Hague, 1651. Dutchmen often preferred to stay in the mother country rather than venture to the New World. *(Painting by J. Van Goyen, Collection Haags Gemeente-Museum, The Hague)*

What the West India Company had expected from the five original patroonships did not materialize. Few immigrants came to strengthen the colony. Even Rensselaerswijk's population grew slowly. Without substantial profits from the fur trade at their disposal, the patroons were apparently unable to risk the heavy expense of colonization. But even in 1639-1640, when the Company decided to stop monopolizing the fur trade and allow the patroons independence from the Company, the desired scale of growth in population did not occur. The patroon could not be forced to admit more settlers if he decided that his land area had plenty. Furthermore, speculators among the patroons tried to take possession of the best lands in hope of selling them at great profits, which of course delayed settlement.

The West India Company's revised charter of 1640 contained additional provisions to ensure faster population growth in New Netherland. Private individuals were now given the opportunity "to choose and take possession of as much land as they can properly cultivate and hold in full ownership." But again no great numbers of immigrants arrived. There was a slight increase when the Company and the city of Amsterdam in The Netherlands agreed that skippers had been charging too much for trans-Atlantic transportation and ordered them to lower their fare by 40% "for all people of small means." But since there was little poverty and persecution in The Netherlands, few had any desire to seek a permanent home in New Netherland. Most Dutchmen preferred to stay in the mother country where so much had to be done both in war and peace.

The Company also devised a plan that would bring 150 orphans to the colony. The city of Amsterdam indicated willingness to cooperate in such a scheme, but nonetheless only 23 orphans arrived in four years. Governor Peter Stuyvesant did not encourage the continuation of this plan after some unsatisfactory experiences with the early orphans.

Many of the Dutch fur traders lived on outposts near the Indians rather than in towns and villages. This gave them easier access to the furs, but it also left them prey to Indian attacks.

In spite of all these difficulties, the population of New Netherland did increase. Unfortunately, however, the immigrants who settled in the colony as free agents preferred to scatter far and wide. Only a minority chose to live in towns and villages. The profitable fur trade induced the majority to live close to the suppliers of the fur, the Indians. Such random settlement quickly turned into disaster when the Indians wanted to attack or settlers were caught between rival Indian groups. Scattered farms and trading posts were beyond the Company's defense capacities. Hence Governor Stuyvesant organized several drives to have fortified towns built. The results were rather poor.

The West India Company's struggle to overcome the New Netherlanders' lack of community spirit was not particularly successful since trade and profits had been the goal in this venture for so long. Colonization policies were developed only as an afterthought. When the Company finally realized what it had to do to populate the colony, it was too late.

6. *Peter Stuyvesant*

Peter Stuyvesant (c.1610-1672) was the last of the six governors in charge of New Netherland. None of those before him had been able to make a success of the colony. They failed in part because the West India Company preferred trade to colonization. Stuyvesant did more than his predecessors to strengthen New Netherland as a colony and succeeded in gaining at least some Company support.

Stuyvesant was courageous. In 1644, when he worked for the West India Company as governor of Curaçao and the West Indies, he lost a leg after leading an attack against the Spanish on St. Martin in the Leeward Islands. A year later the Company appointed him governor of the newly combined lands of New Netherland and the West Indies. They paid him a high salary in addition to his room and board. His pay was about three times that of a minister, seven times a school teacher's, and 20 times an army sergeant's, but his responsibilities were enormous. The effort of governing such a huge area in times of war and peace kept Stuyvesant from applying the full weight of his position to colonization. While the mother country struggled for its

Governor **Peter Stuyvesant** (1610-1672).

very survival, it would have been odd for Stuyvesant not to fight the war first. This is why he was unable to institute a truly democratic form of government.

Also, at this time The Netherlands was competing with England and France, the two nations that had reached a basic understanding by dividing between them the entire territory of the New World. It is true that the French never seriously challenged New Netherland. But, even so, French Jesuit missionaries operating among the Indians near Rensselaerswijk combined their church activity with their desire to help establish a French empire. Rightly or wrongly, the Dutch tended to be suspicious of foreigners as long as the mother country was fighting for its life. And most of all, France's ally, James I of England, was giving out patents for areas in New Netherland as if the entire American coast from Massachusetts to the Virginias were his private property.

Although his predecessors had been instructed to trade in New Netherland, Stuyvesant's responsibility included the particular task of changing New Netherland from a trading post into a permanent settlement. Consequently, in his dealing with the settlers and in his attitudes towards them, the governor reflected the spirit and the practice of the mother country.

Seal of the city of New Amsterdam, 1654.

Street in Albany, New York. On the right is the house of Dominie Gideon Schaets, built in 1657. The notched roof-line and decorative brickwork over the doors and windows are typical of seventeenth-century Dutch architecture in Albany.

While the Seven United Provinces of The Netherlands were emerging as an independent state, national policies were unstable. The long war against Spain had taught the Dutch that it was extremely dangerous to weaken its front against the Hapsburg rulers by allowing men of different religious groups to work out their own ideas of state and society. Therefore, by authority of their federal government, the Dutch enforced a degree of public religious unity. The Dutch Reformed Church was the one publicly recognized Church in the state. But each of the seven provinces which made up the Dutch Republic worked out its own solution for minority groups within its boundaries. In doing so, the provinces granted a large measure of freedom.

In America, Stuyvesant could hardly be expected to become a champion of religious liberty if it would weaken the independence of the Dutch Republic and its New Netherland territory. French Catholic missionaries and Independent or Anglican settlers from England habitually claimed any converts as citizens of their mother country. Stuyvesant thus tried to enforce the policy prevailing in the mother country; that is, only the Dutch Reformed Church was given official public recognition and status. By the same token, however, Stuyvesant granted a large degree of freedom to groups that did not demand exact equality with the Reformed Church.

Even during the time of Peter Stuyvesant, New Amsterdam had a cosmopolitan character. As a growing harbor, the city had many places to eat and drink. The Dutch settlers also introduced their sport *kolf* which later became golf. Their *Sint Nikolaas* (Saint Nicholas), honored on December 5, became the Santa Claus of December 25. New Amsterdam was accustomed to a rather relaxed atmosphere and when the city became New York, nothing much changed. New York City still has numerous places to eat, drink, and be merry.

Tablet representing a St. Nicholas legend in which the bishop restores to life three small children. The fourth-century bishop is believed to be the patron saint of boys and young men. In The Netherlands, his feast is celebrated on December 5 as a children's holiday; good children are given toys by St. Nicholas and his servant Black Peter. The English in New York changed the bishop to Santa Claus and moved the feast to the English holiday of Christmas.

In 1664, the English demanded that Peter Stuyvesant give up all of New Netherland. At a burgomasters' meeting, the enraged Stuyvesant crumpled the proclamation.

PART II

New Netherland Under British Rule, 1664-1776

1. *New Amsterdam-New York*

In the 1650's, England and The Netherlands had battled each other to a draw over commercial and naval issues. By 1661, there were rumors of an English military action against New Netherland. A second sea war broke out in 1664. Prior to open hostilities, however, the two maritime giants had engaged in numerous skirmishes. For instance, irregular British forces landed on Long Island late in 1663 or early in 1664. Although they were no real threat to New Netherland and soon disappeared, the Dutch made some preparations for military action but lacked the determination and the time to be successful against England.

On August 28, 1664, four British warships anchored near Nyack, New York. In the name of the English king, and the Duke of York, Commander Richard Nicholls demanded from Governor Stuyvesant not only New Amsterdam but all of New Netherland. In vain, the Dutch tried to delay by negotiation.

On September 4, the English landed part of their forces near Gravesend on Long Island. The few soldiers that New Amsterdam had were no match for the large English forces that were supported by New Englanders, Indian warriors, and even French pirates, all bent on looting New Amsterdam. The citizens did not want to fight but Stuyvesant did not want to lose his honor by failure to resist the British invasion. Finally, the citizens got him to agree that it would be futile and self-destructive to fight.

Stuyvesant surrenders, September 6, 1664. The Dutch did not have the military strength to repel the English and disregard the English demand.

On September 6, 1664, New Amsterdam surrendered under rather mild terms. Two days later, Peter Stuyvesant ratified the 23 articles of capitulation, his last act as governor of New Netherland. That same Monday, the British forces marched peacefully into New Amsterdam.

Although public officers were now required to swear allegiance to King Charles II, the new subjects of the British Crown were allowed to elect their own administrators. Furthermore, the Dutch were to be free to keep their Reformed Church. Since Nicholls was a wise governor who did not press hard bargains, the British soon won the confidence of the different nationalities that made up the population. The colonists accepted changing the name of their town to New York City, in honor of the Duke of York. With typical Dutch business instinct, the councilors of New York wrote to the Duke and requested that the newly annexed area be granted the trading privileges under the British Navigation Acts. Such an arrangement would give former New Amsterdam access to profitable trade with England. It was for trade that New Amsterdam had been founded; when it became New York it continued to trade. The city would never lose that characteristic.

The West India Company recalled Peter Stuyvesant to The Netherlands in May 1665. The ex-governor went, since he did not feel that his relationship with the Company had come to an end. The councilors with whom he had governed New Amsterdam and who now governed New York issued a certificate to him stating that Stuyvesant had been "a real patriot and a lover of his province." But Stuyvesant loved "his" colony so much that in 1668 he returned to New York. There he lived on his *bouwerij,* or farm, until his death in 1672. The Bowery, the New York street which gives the area its name, was once a road to Stuyvesant's farm.

The Bowery in New York was formerly a road leading to Peter Stuyvesant's farm. In Dutch, a farm is called a *bouwerij.*

Admiral Michiel de Ruyter (1607-1676) spent his life in the Dutch mercantile and naval service. He fought in all three of the seventeenth-century Dutch wars with England.

England and The Netherlands went to war for a third time in 1672. In Britain, Lord Shaftesbury demanded that the Dutch, "the eternal enemy," should now be destroyed. But the Dutch navy, under the famous admiral Michiel de Ruyter, was strong enough to resist. The Dutch could even afford to send a force to the West. Commanded by Admiral Cornelis Evertsen, popularly known as "little Keith the Devil," a Dutch fleet of 23 ships recaptured New York in 1673 and promptly renamed it New Orange. All of New Netherland was claimed for the Dutch Republic. The citizens now had to swear an oath of allegiance to the Dutch federal government.

A Dutch warship of the mid-seventeenth century.

But the British came back after 14 months, without firing a gun. At the Peace of Westminster, The Netherlands was allowed to keep the West Indies, but it had to return New Netherland to England. When the English again assumed control of the colony, Dutch citizens were not granted the privileges of 1664, nor even the rights of the Dutch Reformed Church. Later, when the Assembly of New York met at Albany in 1693, the representatives were therefore well within their rights in establishing the Church of England, now the Protestant Episcopal Church, as the state church. This meant that all non-Episcopalians had to pay a tax in support of the Episcopal Church in addition to whatever they cared to give to their own denomination. Thus the British tried to anglicize their regained colony. And until the American Revolution of 1776, this arrangement did not change.

Sir George Carteret lands in East Jersey. His colony was thought to have more political and religious toleration than was prevalent in New York.

During this period a number of Dutchmen preferred to leave the colony and move into the Raritan Valley in New Jersey. Governor Carteret was more lenient than his colleague in New York. But some Dutchmen thought that even Carteret would be too much for them. They booked passage aboard two ships that took them away from the area to St. James Island in South Carolina. There they began a new life. Thus the tensions in New York disappeared and the remaining Dutch settled down under British rule. However, now that an enemy had conquered New Netherland, still fewer Dutch emigrants cared to settle in the area.

Theodore Frelinghuysen was the second Dutch Reformed pastor to settle in New Jersey. The people of Raritan had formerly been without any religious leadership. Frelinghuysen tried to combat their indifference with a strict standard of moral reform and public penance.

2. *The Dutch Reformed Church*

In 1720, Theodore J. Frelinghuysen, a Dutch minister, came to New Jersey where he was installed as pastor of the Dutch Reformed Church at Raritan. His evangelistic activities soon made him well known. With his Presbyterian neighbor, Gilbert Tennent, he pioneered the Great Awakening that in the 1730's, under Jonathan Edwards, swept the American Middle Colonies.

Although all ministers from "home" were not as well known as Frelinghuysen, they did keep the ties between The Netherlands and its former colony alive. Since the British had granted the Dutch Reformed Church a large degree of independence, it was able to survive and grow. Contact with The Netherlands was maintained not only by Dutch pastors coming to serve in America, but also by young American candidates for the ministry who went to The Netherlands to be ordained and who sometimes stayed to pursue graduate studies.

The so-called "Duke's Laws" declared by the British tolerated no pastor in the colony unless he had been properly ordained in England or another Protestant country. This was one method used by the British to secure the unity of the colony and the stability of their influence.

Gualterius du Bois (left) and **Hendricus Boel**. Du Bois was a *Coetus* leader, working to free the Dutch Reformed Church in America from Netherlands' control. Boel, a leader of the *Conferentie*, was in favor of maintaining ties with The Netherlands.

The requirement was no hardship for those Dutchmen who wanted to keep the old ties with The Netherlands alive. But the long journey across the Atlantic was so hazardous that candidates for the ministry were sometimes lost at sea. For instance, two sons of Theodore Frelinghuysen, Ferdinand and Jacobus, died of smallpox on their return trip from The Netherlands after having been ordained in 1753. Gradually, a group of pastors that became known as the *Coetus* organized itself to press for greater independence from the Church in The Netherlands. They demanded the right to ordain American candidates in the colony and to introduce English in formal worship. Pastor Gualterius du Bois of New York City was one of the strong leaders of the group.

The opponents of this idea allied themselves, too, by forming the so-called *Conferentie*. Led by pastors Hendricus Boel and Johannes Ritzema, the group advocated ties with The Netherlands and ordination there, as well as the continued use of the Dutch language in formal worship. The evangelistic pastor Frelinghuysen, with his burning concern for his flock, supported the Coetus idea of more and greater freedom to act without approval from The Netherlands. The members of the Conferentie tended toward a rather formal style of worship and a degree of aloofness in their pastorates.

The Reformed Church in The Netherlands urged moderation and tried to establish peace between the two parties. But the Reformed Church in the New World needed to make very firm decisions if it was to survive in the English-speaking world. The situation reached a point where harmony between Coetus and Conferentie was no longer feasible. In 1764, the Coetus won a tactical victory when the Reformed Church in New York City installed pastor Archibald Ladlie in its congregation. He was the Reformed Church's first pastor to conduct services in English. Unfortunately, this adjustment came so late that the Reformed Church would never be able to catch up with the growing colony. Eight years later, in 1772, the Reformed Church in The Netherlands finally worked out a plan for reuniting Coetus and Conferentie. But by that time the American Revolution was about to cause even greater changes in the relationship between the Dutch and the American parts of the Reformed Church.

Meanwhile, the British profited most of all. The fundamental split between the Coetus and the Conferentie made it impossible for the Dutch Reformed Church to become a rallying point for those discontented with the British. Thus The Netherlands ceased to be a threat to England in the New World. The American settlers were reaching the point where they would decide among themselves how to run their affairs.

3. *Quakers and Labadists*

Two remarkable groups of Dutch immigrants organized settlements in the Middle Colonies under British rule. The larger one was composed of Quakers, the smaller of Labadists.

Between 1683 and 1690, Dutch Quakers founded Germantown near Philadelphia, Pennsylvania. At the time the territory was known as West New Jersey and belonged to the Duke of York. His daughter Mary was married to the Dutch Prince William III of Orange who became King of England after the Glorious Revolution of 1688. William Penn was personally acquainted with Princess Mary. He visited her in The Netherlands where Penn's mother was born and raised. With

Dutch Prince **William III of Orange** (1650-1702). He became king of England after the Glorious Revolution of 1688.

the assistance of the Princess's father, the Duke of York, Penn obtained the territory for his "holy experiment" in America: a city of brotherly love, Philadelphia.

The name Germantown is misleading, for all but 10 of the 175 immigrants who established the town were of recent Dutch descent and had lived in the Palatinate in Germany prior to emigration to America. Most of their ancestors were Dutch Mennonites. After 1700, these Dutchmen were no match for the number of German settlers that came. However, the original settlers will never be forgotten. In 1688, they drew up and signed the first declaration against slavery:

> There is a saying that we should do to all men like as we will be done ourselves, making no difference of what generation, descent, or color they are. And those who steal, or rob men, and those who buy or purchase them, are they not all alike? Here is liberty of conscience, which is right and reasonable; here ought to be likewise liberty of the body, except for evil doers, which is another case.

Later, in 1758, the Quakers officially decided to expel from their membership anyone who bought or sold slaves.

Unlike the Dutch Quakers at Germantown who came for the holy experiment, the Labadists wanted to withdraw from the world rather than reform it. Therefore they formed an exclusive colony that finally settled at Wieuwerd in The Netherlands. They followed the teachings of the Frenchman Jean de Labadie, a former Jesuit, who had come to The Netherlands where he insisted that a Reformed Church ought to

Mennonite Meetinghouse, Germantown, Pennsylvania. Built in 1770, it is still used today. The original settlers of Germantown were Dutchmen who had lived in Germany prior to their emigration to America.

be absolutely pure. His group often had to move because of local resentment of its strange customs in communal living. Although the colony did not disband when De Labadie died in 1674, communal life was difficult with insufficient money. When the colony decided to disband and to try settling elsewhere, some members emigrated to the Dutch colony, Surinam, in South America. Others looked for new land in America. August Hermann, originally of the West India Company, sold one of his estates, Bohemia Manor, in Maryland to two Labadist scouts from The Netherlands. In 1683, the Labadist immigrants began to arrive. By 1700, the colony numbered approximately 100 persons.

The Labadists held all goods in common. When entering the community, a member had to put his belongings in the common stock. Though one was free to leave at any time, nobody was allowed to take back "his" property. However, the colonists did not unfailingly practice their high ideals. Although they were officially opposed to slavery, the Labadists could not resist the temptation to buy slaves to help them plant corn, flax, and hemp. And while the community officially condemned smoking, it did plant hundreds of acres of tobacco for profit.

In earlier times, the Labadists each had to take turns at the washtub, a practice which they called "pride's funeral," for they felt that everyone should share in the humblest tasks. But life at Bohemia Manor, or the *Labadie Tract* as it became known, failed to conquer pride. When in 1698 the communal holdings were broken up in individually owned parcels of land, director Schlütter gave himself a fourth of all the lands. By 1727, the Labadists no longer formed a community. Escape from the world was apparently not so easy; for these Labadists it had proved to be impossible.

4. *The Net Result*

In the period from 1664 until 1776, few Dutch immigrants arrived in America. The Netherlands prospered economically. There was little need for emigration. Besides, the Dutch republic guaranteed a large degree of liberty to its citizens and to refugees. Very few, if any, left to gain a larger degree of religious or political freedom. The earlier Dutch settlers in America maintained themselves as a group unaided by an influx of new immigrants. Even the attractive picture presented in letters from the new settlers did not increase emigration from The Netherlands.

Stephen Van Cortlandt (1643-1700) became prosperous in New York. In 1697, he was granted a royal patent which named his estates a manor and himself as lord of the manor. The largest part of his estates covered 87,000 acres and extended for 10 miles on the east bank of the Hudson River, just north of Manhattan.

Van Cortlandt Manor House, built in 1681. It has been restored and now serves as a museum.

It has been estimated that the Dutch population at the time New Amsterdam surrendered in 1663 numbered approximately 10,000.

Americans of Dutch Extraction, 1790

(Figures obtained from The Atlantic Migration, *by Marcus Hansen, specialist in American immigration history.)*

Connecticut	600
Delaware	2,000
Georgia	100
Kentucky	600
Maine	100
Maryland	1,000
Massachusetts	600
New Hampshire	100
New Jersey	35,000
New York	55,000
North Carolina	800
Pennsylvania	7,500
Rhode Island	250
South Carolina	500
Tennessee	600
Vermont	500
Virginia	1,500
Total population	106,750

PART III

The Dutch and the American Revolution, 1776-1815

1. *Changes and Continuing Contacts*

Great changes took place in America and in The Netherlands between 1776 and 1815. The British colonies successfully rebelled to establish the United States of America. While France significantly aided the rebels in America, it had no respect for Dutch independence and for a time, from 1810 until 1813, even incorporated the United Provinces as part of the French Empire. During this period America began its rise to world power, but The Netherlands lost its prominent rank among the nations.

There were significant contacts between America and The Netherlands in spite of the changes now taking place. As in earlier times, the two countries were more related by trade than by migration. Dutch emigrants to America had been few indeed, but Dutchmen and American colonists had engaged in brisk trade. For instance in 1757, Governor Hardy reported that New York City and Amsterdam traded so intensely in tea, linen, and gunpowder and arms for the Indians that it "almost totally discouraged the importation of these commodities from Great Britain." The method of trade varied from legitimate importing to outright smuggling.

The Dutch, however, were never in a position to overtake the British in American trade, for the Netherlanders lacked a well-organized and widely varied industry. Dutch merchants specialized far more in financing of trade and in banking operations than in the manufacture of goods needed in America. With the exception of sugar, tobacco, and gin, Dutch products were unable to compete in the world of trade. While other countries adopted tariff walls to aid their industries, The Netherlands refused the demands of the Dutch manufacturers for protective tariffs. Even if the industrialists' view had been adopted as national policy, the merchants would still have been unwilling to risk their capital in reviving domestic industries. The merchants preferred to invest money in all types of trade and shipping. Hence they happily participated in and profited from the many ways Americans and foreigners eluded the British Navigation Acts. Parliament had passed these acts to protect British trade. The acts required the use of English ships and crews, and that many products be shipped to and from the colonies via England.

Peter Gansevoort (1749-1812). During the Revolutionary War, Gansevoort commanded Fort Schuyler. In the Saratoga campaign, he defended the post against the British. Fort Schuyler protected an important route from the Hudson to Lake Ontario.

2. *American Revolution*

At the outbreak of revolution in America, Dutch merchants were overjoyed with the prospect of supplying the new Republic with the industrial products it needed. Dutch industry hoped to gain access to the markets that had been monopolized by England for so long. Dutch bankers prepared to advance the huge sums of money America would need.

St. Eustatius, a small island in the Dutch West Indies, became the center for illegal trade between The Netherlands and America. The island was ideally situated. In answer to British complaints, the Dutch pointed out that St. Eustatius had always depended on American supplies for food and therefore welcomed American ships. This was true, but the Dutch didn't say that they also engaged in the profitable rum-slave-molasses trade with the Americans. The Dutch were fully prepared to rake in profits by increasing trade with the rebels.

On December 16, 1776, St. Eustatius's Dutch governor, Johan de Graeff, fired his guns 13 times in reply to the salute from the *Andrea Doria,* the first trader flying the American flag to enter the harbor. The British were enraged. Their protests embarrassed the Dutch government enough to recall De Graeff. But he was cleared and reinstated after presenting his reports. The British were not at all satisfied. Flying an American flag, the British Admiral George Rodney attacked and conquered the island in 1778. Then he continued to fly the Dutch flag over the island. He thus trapped many American and other ships carrying illegal goods. It was a fabulous victory for the British, especially because of the vast stores of strategic materials on the island. But this conquest also signaled another war between England and The Netherlands.

3. *The Dutch Dilemma*

The family ties between the Dutch House of Orange and the British royal family had usually helped to smooth relations between the two countries. At this time, however, the Dutch merchants preferred trade with American rebels to good relations with the British.

And while William V of Orange tried to steer a pro-British course, Dutch businessmen, especially those in Amsterdam, wanted the Estates-General, or Parliament, to arrive at an understanding with the revolutionaries in America.

The American colonies had to finance their rebellion. The state of South Carolina, for instance, used the financial influence of two recent immigrants from The Netherlands: Pieter LePoole and Alexander Gillon. They had left their native Rotterdam in peacetime to come to America, where they had done well in business and now supported the revolution. LePoole used his connections with Jan Westendorp, a merchant in Amsterdam, to raise credit for South Carolina. Alexander Gillon actually went to The Netherlands, in March 1778, to borrow money as an advance for the tobacco and rice South Carolina would ship to Amsterdam.

Dutch merchants were risking the wrath of the British if they aided the American rebels. On the other hand, France had aided the revolutionaries from the start and by exchanging ambassadors had recognized the new Republic in 1778. France even fought on the side of the Americans. In order to win against Britain, the French government exerted strong pressure on the Dutch merchants to support the American cause. The Dutch found themselves in quite a dilemma. Under British rule, they had been granted trading privileges with the colonies. However, if Britain should win in America, these privileges would be lost if the Dutch did not support England. On the other hand, the Americans would certainly not favor those who had opposed their battle for freedom. The ambassadors of France and England in The Hague bent over backward competing for Dutch support.

When Benjamin Franklin was ambassador in Paris, he appointed Charles Frederic Guillaume Dumas as his agent in The Netherlands. Dumas promptly selected De La Lande and Fynje in Amsterdam as the banking firm to handle American finances. But Franklin himself preferred to do business in The Netherlands with the firm of Horneca and Fizeaux, also at Amsterdam, because this banking house was a subsidiary of Grand, the large financial firm in Paris. Thus the Americans tried to gain access to the Dutch capital that traditionally had favored investment in Great Britain. Those who preferred France and those who sympathized with the American cause were willing to risk a change. They wanted to be careful, however, not to antagonize Great Britain unnecessarily.

Americans tried in all possible ways to get capital. Alexander Gillon from South Carolina and William Lee of Virginia were but two of the Americans who promised to ship American goods to Dutch merchants paying in advance. A number of Amsterdam firms were willing to take risks in order to take over part of the American trade which had been exclusively British.

In 1780, Dutch-American **John Paulding** and two associates intercepted British spy, Major John Andre, who was returning from the American lines. While searching Andre, they found that he carried a plan of the fortifications for West Point as well as other documents given him by Benedict Arnold. The men refused Andre's bribes and arrested him. This act led to the discovery of Arnold as a spy.

William V delivers the American-Dutch treaty draft to the Assembly of the Estates-General, 1780. According to the treaty, Dutch merchants would give financial support to the Americans fighting the Revolution.

4. A Secret Treaty

Jean de Neufville went the farthest of all. With William Lee of Virginia he worked out the so-called Treaty of Aachen, or Aix-la-Chapelle. It was a secret treaty between the city of Amsterdam and America in which Amsterdam merchants pledged financial support to the Americans. Unfortunately, the British got a copy of it when they captured the ship carrying the American ambassador Henry Laurens off the coast of Newfoundland in 1780. The former president of the Continental Congress was carrying the document with him.

England was now in a position to put enormous pressure on its official ally, William V of Orange. But the Dutch parliament stood firm and accepted Amsterdam's explanation of the Treaty. The British

Both **Henry Laurens** (1724-1792) and **John Adams** (1735-1826) served as American ambassadors to The Netherlands.

recalled their ambassador Yorke from The Hague. War with England was now inevitable. As William V had warned in 1778, the Dutch Republic would now become dependent upon France.

The American cause did not seem very promising at this time. Charleston was lost, General Gates had been defeated, and Benedict Arnold had betrayed the revolution. Nevertheless, John Adams, who replaced Laurens as American ambassador to The Netherlands, gained the confidence of several moneylenders, especially after the six reluctant Dutch provinces followed Friesland's example and recognized the American colonies as an independent nation (1782). By that time, Adams had already scored his first major success in obtaining a loan of five million guilders from the Estates-General. It is true that the money was officially lent to France, but it was understood that King Louis XVI was to use it for the Americans. Adams's greatest success came at the close of the war when three banking firms at Amsterdam, De La Lande and Fynje, together with the Van Staphorst Brothers and the Willinks, combined to extend a five-million-guilder loan at the low rate of 5% to the new American republic. It is interesting to note that Sweden, Russia, and Poland paid much higher rates for money loaned them. Only the Austrian emperor paid less. By 1795, the Dutch had invested more than 30 million guilders in the United States.

Pieter van Berckel, the first Dutch ambassador
to the United States, addresses the Congress at
Princeton, 1782.

After recognizing the new American state, the Republic of the
Seven United Provinces sent as its first ambassador, Pieter Johan van
Berckel, a former mayor of Rotterdam. He arrived in America with
his party in July of 1783.

The link between The Netherlands and the United States remained
weak, however. At this time, few Dutchmen emigrated to America. By
contrast, the Danish king issued a decree against emigration because
so many Danes had left for America. The situation in The Netherlands
made emigration unnecessary: food and work were available to
practically all people, and individual liberties were guaranteed by
custom and law. Although John Adams had reported earlier that many
Dutchmen had expressed a desire to emigrate, few did.

At the close of the American Revolution, the Dutch merchants and
manufacturers believed that England had lost the profitable markets
in its former colonies for good. What American would want to trade
with the enemy? But the Dutch business world had failed to see future
implications in the fact that many British firms had been actively

trading with the American rebels through daughter firms on the European continent. Of the 22 tobacco dealers in Rotterdam, for example, no less than 14 were British firms dealing in American tobacco. The Dutch simply underestimated the power of the Industrial Revolution to transform England into a vast supply house which could make a host of superior products available to the world. Besides, British capital was so powerful that American businessmen were granted credit terms not available anywhere else. For instance, when the Revolution began, British bankers had advanced nearly four million pounds on future crops of Southern planters. And although the British lost part of their colonies in America, they suffered few economic losses when the war ended because they again offered the Americans very liberal terms.

There was not much to gain for the Dutch, who were unable to match Britain's spectacular rise in industry. Of course, they tried. Perhaps the most pathetic effort was made by the Society of Patriots at Enkhuizen. They shipped vats of salted herring to George Washington and Governor Jonathan Trumbull of Massachusetts, in the hope that the United States would import Dutch herring on a regular basis. The noisiest effort must have been the party organized by the brewers of Schiedam in honor of John Adams. They wanted him to taste their liquors and thereby gain access to the American market. It is not clear how much Adams did contribute, but Schiedam and its brewers have prospered ever since.

5. *Dutch Money in America*

The Dutch continued to export capital to America. Attracted by the high rate of interest — 14% in the first year and from 10% to 22% thereafter — the Dutch bought shares issued by the Bank of North America.

Silver medal of 1782, made by the States of Friesland to recognize the United States Declaration of Independence.

The English did not take full advantage of such impressive interest rates. They were busy investing capital in their own rapidly expanding industry. England made its profits in America by selling its products to the Americans. At this time, Dutch industry was no match for the British. Whatever products the Dutch made for export, British industry soon matched in quality and at lower prices. As James Madison stated in 1785: "Our trade was never more completely monopolized by Great Britain."

Meanwhile, the Dutch bankers channeled investment money to America. The U.S. Board of Treasury reported in 1788 that the Dutch held $2,501,176 of their listed foreign contributions of $2,768,839. The returns were impressive, but only for the Dutch bankers. Dutch businessmen found it impossible in their own country to compete for the capital needed to modernize and mechanize their industries.

By cooperating with pre-revolutionary Dutch trading firms in New York, the investment houses in The Netherlands participated actively in the building of America. Very few people were needed to operate the intense financial relations between America and The Netherlands. The four main Dutch banking houses appointed only one agent, Theophile Cazenove, as their full-time representative in the United States.

Cazenove checked carefully into the financial condition of each individual state, since all of them needed new capital as urgently as did the Federal Government in Washington. Numerous schemes to improve roads and inland navigation were competing for attention. Also, Cazenove could not possibly ignore the vast acreages the states were making available to settlers.

Cazenove's employers showed no interest in this type of project until their agent sent them samples of maple sugar from northern New York. Dutch sugar refiners were so impressed with the quality of this product that in 1791, a combination of five firms delegated Gerrit Boon to start producing maple sugar. Boon bought more than 30,000 acres on the West Canada Creek, an arm of the Mohawk River. He promptly hired Yankee carpenters and constructed a new settlement where the Cincinnati and Steuben Creeks met. The new industry was not a financial success and had to be abandoned. But the new settlement, called Barnevelt, still remains.

Barnevelt became one of the centers for offices of the Holland Land Company. Upon the recommendation of Cazenove and Boon, the Company (also known as the Club of Six because of the six participating trading firms) invested money in land in western New York and northern Pennsylvania. Since these lands were to be sold at a profit, more than one center was required where the Company could do business. The building of additional centers prevented Barnevelt from growing into a large company town.

Where the Buffalo Creek empties into Lake Erie, the Club of Six laid out a new settlement, later known as Buffalo. However, the expense of the necessary harbor work prevented it from becoming an important Dutch town. Even though the construction of the Erie Canal attracted many immigrants, few of them were Dutch.

6. *The Patriotten and Emigration*

Late in the eighteenth century, it seemed as though the territory of the Holland Land Company might attract larger numbers of Dutch immigrants. Political unrest developed in The Netherlands after Great Britain made peace with the Americans and could compel America's Dutch ally to sign a very unfavorable peace treaty (1784). The Dutch were now asking themselves: Should they support the democratic ideals that were gaining favor in France and the United States? Or should they favor the more autocratic rule of the House of Orange as worked out by Prince William V and the aristocracy? The democratic *Patriotten* naturally looked to France for leadership. A strong spokesman among them was Francois Adriaan Van der Kemp, a Mennonite pastor.

In 1787, Van der Kemp and his fellow Patriotten decided they were strong enough to take over the government and make democratic changes that the Orange Party did not want, as yet. But Prussia's king came to the aid of Prince William V of Orange, whose wife was the king's sister. The Patriotten were no match for the Prussian soldiers. Those who did not leave The Netherlands as the Prussian army marched in, left later when the victorious Orange Party began a policy of repression and punishment.

Thousands of Patriotten fled to France, but very few came to the United States. These political exiles felt that it would not be long before they could return to a liberated Netherlands. It would be far easier to do so from France than from America. But revolution did not come to The Netherlands until eight years later, in 1795. It was promptly called a "velvet revolution" because no lives were lost on either side. Van der Kemp was among the small number of Patriotten who decided to go to America between 1787 and 1795. John Adams, America's ambassador in The Hague, provided Van der Kemp with the proper introductions to Benjamin Franklin, George Washington, and Jeremiah Wadsworth. Adams called Van der Kemp "a star of the first magnitude."

Unfortunately, Van der Kemp's farm near Esopus (Kingston, New York) failed. By 1797, the Van der Kemps had moved to Barnevelt and were joined by several other Dutch immigrants. This small settlement knew happy days. Governor DeWitt Clinton requested that Van der Kemp translate New York's colonial records from the Dutch into English. Harvard College thanked him for his intellectual activities by awarding him an honorary Doctor of Laws degree. Adam Gerard Mappa, another member of the community, had a 900-volume library which, in addition to Van der Kemp's, enabled the small isolated band of Dutch liberals to increase their knowledge and understanding.

In 1795, the old Republic of the Seven United Provinces fell, under French pressure. Prince William V of Orange found refuge in England. But the new Batavian Republic, established under close supervision of the French, did not bring the long-awaited democratic improvements. Beginning in 1801, France tried to include The Netherlands as

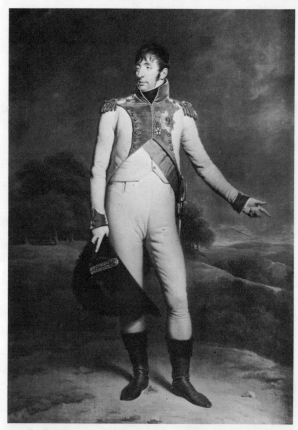

Louis Bonaparte (1778-1846), brother to Napoleon I, ruled The Netherlands from 1806 to 1810.

part of her empire. In 1810 Napoleon annexed the former Republic as a French province. By that time the French had lost the good will of even the staunchest Patriotten. Napoleon's total war against England had brought tight controls that made it virtually impossible to leave The Netherlands for America. For this reason, the small settlement at Barnevelt failed to attract more Dutch immigrants.

7. *The New Kingdom of The Netherlands*

When Napoleon was finally defeated in 1813, the son of Prince William V returned to The Netherlands. Both Orangists and Patriotten gladly accepted him as King William I. Both groups felt that the urgent task of rebuilding the nation had to be accomplished under the new king. As a result of the Vienna Peace Congress of 1815, the Austrian Netherlands, now known as Belgium, and The Netherlands were joined together as an enlarged kingdom under William I. The Netherlands was expected to act as a sentinel on France's northern borders. The Dutch population reacted very favorably to King William's energetic efforts to reconstruct the kingdom. This was especially so since the monarch governed on the rather liberal terms of the Enlightenment, though not as a constitutionally democratic king. Consequently, there were not enough disgruntled liberals in The Netherlands to start a mass movement of emigration to the United States.

Besides, the Club of Six investment firms expected to reap profits by selling their landholdings rather than by creating Dutch colonies. For this reason, they did not engage in vigorous campaigns to lure Dutchmen to settle on their lands. The Club of Six had not been unwilling to promote emigration to the United States, but there were certain facts that naturally worked against Dutch emigration. A considerable amount of money was required to be successful on the new land. In addition, farmers would have to spin, bake, butcher, and do literally everything themselves. Those families who could afford to emigrate were also those least accustomed to doing the manual labor required on a farm. On the other hand, those who were able to do all the work usually didn't have enough money to emigrate.

Of course, the Holland Land Company did not object to Dutch settlers, but it gave them no preferential treatment. The Company was not at all like the West India Company. The Holland Land Company welcomed cash buyers of every nationality, as it was organized mainly for profits. Therefore, neither Barnevelt nor any other settlement of the Company had the kind of backing that would have made these places centers for Dutch settlers.

8. *The Dutch in the New Republic*

Many Americans of Dutch extraction are remembered for their contribution to and their suffering for American independence. Since most of the Dutch Loyalists who had supported England moved to Canada, it became easy to be proud of the Dutch record in the Revolution. Naturally, the Dutch Yankees looked more to their Dutch than to their English past while memories of British oppression were still fresh. It even became fashionable to be Dutch.

The use of the Dutch language in the Middle Colonies had never been entirely lost. People still conversed in Dutch, and in the Dutch Reformed Church sermons were often preached in the Dutch language, although the use of English began to gain quite rapidly after 1800. So it is not surprising to find that in 1835 the Saint Nicholas Society was established to celebrate Santa Claus's arrival in original Dutch fashion on December 5.

Cornelius Vanderbilt (1843-1899). With the family holdings, he helped to establish the Vanderbilt Clinic in New York City. He was the grandson and namesake of Commodore Vanderbilt, who established the family fortune.

57

More efforts were made to preserve the past in forms other than the Dutch language. Those who could afford the time and the money began to trace their ancestry back to Dutch colonial times. They were promptly dubbed Knickerbockers, a nickname for the baggy pants worn by the colonial Dutch. The Knickerbockers formed a very exclusive society. It took the Vanderbilts three generations before they were accepted. Washington Irving, in his *Knickerbocker History of New York*, brought out some of the oddities and the ridiculous characteristics among the early and later Dutch.

The Huguenot Society of America was established much later, in 1883, and the Holland Society of New York in 1885. Their aim was identical: to preserve the relevant Dutch contributions to the history of America. To them, Dutch referred to all who had come to New Netherland, even though their origins had not been in The Netherlands.

William I (1772-1843) tried unsuccessfully to unite Catholic Belgium and Protestant Holland.

PART IV

The Great Migration, 1815-1860

1. *William I's Kingdom*

In the reorganized Europe of 1815, King William I tried his utmost to unify Belgium, primarily a Catholic country, with The Netherlands, where Protestantism prevailed. Both countries had begun to practice a larger degree of religious toleration while they were dominated by a revolutionary France. But the past could not be easily eradicated, especially since religious devotion had been so closely connected with nationalistic sentiments.

King William was willing to grant the Roman Catholics in Belgium freedom of worship and the rights of free citizens. But the Protestants in the North would never permit him to establish Catholicism as the religion of the state. On the other hand, King William could never allow the Protestant North to dominate Catholic Belgium.

The King was convinced that the economic survival of his new realm would depend on rapid industrial growth. He used his power to promote large-scale industrialization, but in so doing he had to overcome ancient customs and prejudices. At this point, William felt that a democracy would result in increased opposition to industrialization and thus endanger the economic foundations upon which the state had to be built.

By 1830, the liberal or democratic element united with the Roman Catholics in a drive for greater independence from the King. Aided by France, which wanted to reduce the strength of the watchdog in the north, the Belgians rebelled against William, who had just concluded a mutually satisfactory agreement with the Pope. The northern part of the Kingdom quickly rallied behind William. Their successful march into the Belgian part was stopped, however, when first France and later England began to aid the Belgians. King William waited in vain for the Holy Alliance to come to his aid. After nine long and expensive years of mobilization and readiness for war, King William finally agreed to the separation of Belgium as an independent state. But he also resigned, leaving the throne to his son, King William II (1840). It was the son who consented to considerable democratic reforms and effected significant improvements in relations between Catholics and Protestants.

2. *Emigration As a Way Out*

The many tensions in The Netherlands caused Dutchmen to consider alternate courses of action; among them was the possibility of emigration. The following table shows that the number deciding to leave for the United States increased, but at a slow rate.

Emigration Pattern from The Netherlands to America, 1820-1865

Based on United States Government statistics

1820-1824	215
1825-1829	890
1830-1834	528
1835-1839	849
1840-1844	1,115
1845-1849	6,509
1850-1854	4,889
1855-1859	6,233
1860-1865	2,190
Total	23,418

Father Johannes VandenBroek preached sermons in Dutch, French, German, Indian, and English. He had done missionary work among German immigrants and Indians, as well as among the Dutch in America.

Some individuals left The Netherlands for America because further democratic reforms came much too slowly for them. Without such reforms, they felt, the economy would never return to normal. But since reforms did take place and the House of Orange continued to be very popular, relatively few Dutch liberals decided to leave for the United States.

A Catholic emigration to the Fox River Valley in Wisconsin guided by Father Johannes VandenBroek, between 1847 and 1850, was far more numerous. Although King William II had adopted a conciliatory religious policy, the Roman Catholics in The Netherlands were unable to push through their "Belgian" demand for Catholic schools. Some Catholics were distressed enough by this failure to leave the country. Additional Catholics joined the group because their latent desire to emigrate had been triggered by economic difficulties in The Netherlands after the Belgian revolt. But even these migrants never reached the proportions of the *New Migration* in which sharply increased numbers of Protestants began to leave The Netherlands.

An 1856 view of Little Chute along the Fox River, Wisconsin. Little Chute was founded in 1848 by Father VandenBroek. By the end of the year, a telegraph line had been established, and by 1855, the settlement had a canal connection with the industrial center of Kaukauma. St. John's Church was a focal point in the community.

3. *The New Migration*

Although relatively few Dutchmen actually emigrated, the entire population was greatly concerned about the welfare of their country whose future had to be newly charted. The sterner Protestants were distressed when King William I began to pacify the Roman Catholics. The Belgian revolt convinced them that Catholics were very poor patriots. They explained the economic ills of the country as the logical consequence of divine punishment upon a Netherlands that had given up the old ways prevailing in The Netherlands prior to 1795. These stern Protestants had deep misgivings about what they called "superficial Christianity" being taught in the public schools. Nor did they trust the modern, optimistic preaching, quite frequently heard in the old Reformed Church—that Christ was a Teacher and Educator, and in that sense a Savior.

Instead, this concerned group wanted a revival of the preaching and liturgy that had prevailed earlier. They wanted the Dutch Reformed Church fully restored to the privileged position she had held prior to the French Revolution and its aftermath in The Netherlands. Even the principle of constitutional government was repulsive to them. In their opinion the king ought to be solely responsible to God. Thus they urged King William I to abolish the constitution. And they did so at the very time that the democratic forces in both Belgium and The Netherlands were pressing hard for further constitutional reforms.

A break with the Reformed Church was inevitable. In 1834, the Christian Seceded Church broke away and provided a new denomination for the discontented. The courts rejected their claim to the property of the Reformed Church to which they felt entitled on the basis of their loyalty to doctrine and practice of the past.

By 1840 most Seceders had given up their claim to the property of the Reformed Church. Succeeding his father, King William II adopted more tolerant policies toward them. But the nation, now without Belgium, was sharply split. The Seceders were a minority of perhaps 30,000 in a population of over two million. The great majority of Seceders were laborers, peasants, and small farmers. When the potato blight struck The Netherlands early in the 1840's, the working class, which depended almost exclusively upon the potato for its staple food,

King **William II** (1792-1849) faced the financial crisis of the potato blight by raising a "voluntary loan" among the people. During his reign, he granted considerable constitutional reform.

was especially hard hit. Food riots occurred in the province of Friesland. In the province of Gelderland scores of people starved to death. The limited funds of the Christian Seceded Church were taxed beyond capacity as poverty-stricken members had nowhere else to turn for survival. The employment situation had become desperate, too. While in 1841 more than 13% of the population was on relief, by 1850 the number had climbed to over 27%.

Under these circumstances, emigration seemed an attractive solution. If many Dutch people left their homeland, it would be easier to provide food and employment for those who remained. In 1839, the Ministry of Colonies began to promote emigration to Surinam, a Dutch colony in South America. Conditions had finally become ripe for a large-scale migration. But the project in Surinam failed. The migration began in 1854, but over 189 of the 384 immigrants died within the first six months.

Although the disaster was blamed more on the tropical climate than on the poor planning, the Dutch Minister of Colonies, Jean C. Baud, did not want to permit the Seceded Church to establish emigrant colonies in either the West or the East Indies. The suffering people did not wait for the Minister of Colonies to change his mind. Many individuals began to leave. One of them, Alexander Hartgerink, was a friend of the two Seceded pastors at Arnhem, Anthony Brummelkamp and his brother-in-law, Albertus C. Van Raalte. Hartgerink, who arrived in the United States in 1845, wrote back to the two pastors, confirming the reports received from earlier settlers that conditions in America were indeed excellent. So Brummelkamp and Van Raalte began to organize a Society of Christians for the Dutch Emigration to the United States. They published a pamphlet under the title: *Emigration: or Why Do We Promote Emigration to North America and not to Java* (in the Dutch East Indies). Within a year, it had gone through four reprints. The Seceders, however, did not all agree that emigration was the answer. Many felt it necessary to remain in The Netherlands in order to press for ultimate adoption of their viewpoint.

An additional social factor played a very strong role in the new migration. Even when France's domination of The Netherlands ended, the differences between classes — nobleman and commoner, master and servant, rich and poor — were very obvious. America as the common man's utopia appealed to those whose equality before the law was not matched by equality in the economy and social structure of the country. Therefore, it is no accident that pastors Brummelkamp and Van Raalte included J. A. Beukenhorst's letter from America in one of their publications about emigration to the United States. The letter stated that "The poor here are worth as much as the rich; one need not raise one's hat to anybody. Rich people honor us because we work for them..."

4. *To the Faithful in the United States of America*

Brummelkamp and Van Raalte had organized an effective emigration society. In May 1846 they bought tickets to the United States for three destitute families, a party of 13, who landed a month later in Boston. Since their first task was to find employment, these families were unable to act as scouts for those ready to come, but the next group of 11 families had sufficient finances of their own to travel farther inland. By rail, canal boat, and steamboat they journeyed to Milwaukee. From there, most of them went on to Sheboygan County, Wisconsin.

This group had with them a letter written by Brummelkamp and Van Raalte addressed *To the Faithful in the United States of North America*. It was an eloquent plea to Christians in America to extend

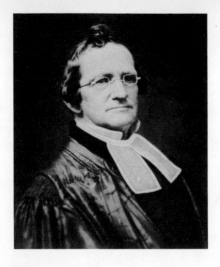

Dr. Isaac Newton Wyckoff (1792-1869) served as pastor of the Second Dutch Reformed Church at Albany, New York, from 1836 to 1866. He helped to organize many immigrant aid societies.

a helping hand to the Dutch migrants now leaving The Netherlands. This letter was presented to Dr. Isaac N. Wyckoff, pastor of the Second Reformed Church at Albany, New York. Wyckoff had an English version of the letter published in the October 16, 1846, issue of the *Christian Intelligencer,* official publication of the Dutch Reformed Church. In response to the letter, the Church formed emigrant aid societies.

Cheaper transatlantic passage made migration easier after 1815. This had resulted from an increase in shipping on the Atlantic Ocean. American cotton, rice, tobacco, grain, and other products were brought to Europe. Henry Clay's American System, adopted in 1816, levied a 25% tariff on imported goods to protect the infant industries of America. Hence many American ships found no return cargo after bringing their wares from America to Europe. Rather than sailing the return trip empty, skippers loaded their ships with immigrants, the one import on which no duties were levied. Westbound passage across the Atlantic could therefore be bought at bargain rates.

A passenger was advised to take 180 lbs. of food with him for the trip. But most immigrants could not afford to buy so much food, especially when lack of food forced them to emigrate. Shortage of proper food was a partial cause of the high death rate aboard the emigrant ships.

5. *Van Raalte's Colony*

Van Raalte had not at first intended to emigrate to America. However, while recovering from typhoid fever, he changed his mind. In September of 1846, Van Raalte and his family sailed from Rotterdam

In 1847, **Albertus C. Van Raalte** founded the Dutch colony at Holland, Michigan.

aboard *The Southerner* with about 100 other Dutch emigrants. In November, they arrived in New York City and were welcomed by Dr. Thomas DeWitt, pastor of the Dutch Reformed Church, who had heeded Wyckoff's call for aid.

Dutchmen in New York City founded the *Netherlands Society for the Protection of Emigrants from Holland* in order "to assist and protect those Netherlanders who may of themselves wish to make this the country of their adoption." The Society offered immigrants lodging at the corner of Cedar and Greenwich Streets for 50 cents a day. Within a year, unfortunately, rivalry between the leaders caused the failure of the society. There were also two other aid societies, but much of their time was spent battling over the innocent immigrants.

Van Raalte and his band did not have to cope with that situation. After only one day of preparation, the company left New York City and sailed up the Hudson to Albany. In spite of Wyckoff's kind reception there, Van Raalte stuck to his goal: to reach Milwaukee by water before the winter set in. But their boat reached Detroit too late. The winter weather had already stopped lake traffic through the Mackinac Straits.

However, due to the kindness of the lawyer Theodore Romeyn, and Pastor Duffield of the Presbyterian Church, Van Raalte's band found shelter and sufficient employment to survive through the winter. Meanwhile, Van Raalte traveled westward to Milwaukee on a scouting trip.

On the way to Milwaukee, he stopped at Kalamazoo, where friends of Romeyn introduced him to Judge John R. Kellogg who had settled in Allegan, Michigan, in 1836. These men convinced Van Raalte that he should accompany Judge Kellogg and his Potawatomi Indian guide

An 1876 map of Michigan, showing the city of Holland along the Black Lake. Van Raalte once said, "I chose this region advisedly because of its great variety of possibilities...In my mind's eye I saw here not only a locality well adapted to the condition of streams of laborers, but I saw also flourishing fisheries, a beautiful harbor...with our own ships together with a rich rural community."

The Log Church was one of the first structures built in the Holland Colony. It was used for services until 1856. In 1858, **Adriaan Zwemer** (1823-1910) became the first Dutch immigrant to be ordained in the Holland Colony as minister of the Reformed Church.

to inspect lands north of the Rabbit and Kalamazoo rivers, around Black Lake, now called Lake Macatawa after the Indian name *Mekatewgamie* (Black Water).

At that time Michigan was eager to attract immigrants. Prominent legislators were appointed to seven area committees to aid migrants from The Netherlands. But Van Raalte hesitated before deciding to bring his group to the wild shores of the Black River rather than to Wisconsin. He finally chose the site of his colony, appropriately called "Holland," along the Black River in southwestern Michigan.

Early in the summer of 1847 the number of settlers in Van Raalte's colony had already increased to over 1,100. The villages of Graafschap, Zeeland, Groningen, Drenthe, Overijsel, Friesland, and others clustering around Holland, had their origin in this period. Van Raalte's ministerial friends in The Netherlands, such as Vander Meulen, Ypma, and Bolks, now personally accompanied their flocks to the Dutch colony. But the process of adapting the forest to human habitation was difficult and could not keep pace with the rapid growth in population.

The first band in Holland, Michigan, 1871.

The swamps and forests through which the Black River made its way were breeding-grounds for illnesses, especially since the settlers lacked proper housing, suitable clothing, and most of all a well-balanced diet. Neither a doctor nor proper medication were available when infectious diseases struck late in the summer of 1847 and continued through 1848. However, in spite of the setbacks, by 1848 the settlement numbered 4,000 and stretched out over 20 miles.

6. *Scholte's Colony*

Van Raalte tried but failed to attract all Dutch immigrants to his colony. Hendrik P. Scholte, his ministerial colleague and fellow-Seceder in The Netherlands, actively campaigned against the Michigan settlement. As late as 1846 Scholte was still opposing emigration from The Netherlands. But the desperate plight of the poor compelled him to change his mind. Arriving in Boston in May 1847, Scholte and a committee of settlers decided to go to Iowa. Their settlement was named Pella, after the Greek Macedonian city of Pella, which in the first century had sheltered refugee Christians. Communally the group

Hendrik P. Scholte led 800 immigrants to Pella, Iowa, in 1847.

bought over 18,000 acres of land, and acquired farm equipment and livestock. Unlike Van Raalte's group, Scholte's followers included many wealthy families, who helped give the colony a good start. Later, Pella got a real boost when the California Gold Rush brought through many travelers who bought their supplies there.

Father VandenBroek's Catholic center in the Fox River Valley of Wisconsin, Van Raalte's Holland, Michigan, and Scholte's Pella, Iowa, attracted most of the Dutch immigrants. In these areas new arrivals were welcomed and efficiently assisted. Nevertheless, not all immigrants from The Netherlands tried to reach these "Dutch" colonies.

Pella, Iowa, prospered from wealthy citizens and from the many travelers who visited the city on their way to California and the gold rush. Scholte's spired house was located on the north side of central park. The corner building still stands as the Pella National Bank.

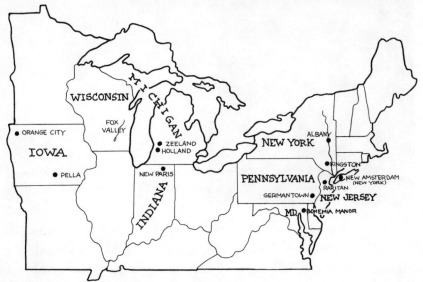

Map of the Dutch settlements in northeastern and north central United States.

7. *Other Settlements*

In 1853, a group of Dutch Mennonites who refused to be inducted for training in the Dutch military service came to New Paris, Indiana. Since there were few Mennonites in The Netherlands, the number of these emigrants was also few. Without a steady stream of newcomers they had no particular reason to remain Dutch. Within 25 years they could not be distinguished from fellow Mennonites among whom they had settled.

A small group from Friesland settled in Lancaster, New York, near Buffalo. They developed a prosperous dairy industry, but were not joined by other Dutchmen since land prices were very high.

The less wealthy were drawn to the three pioneer areas where the churches provided not only spiritual comfort but also the practical means to start a new life. However, economic and social conditions in The Netherlands rapidly improved after 1850, which caused the pressure for emigration to decrease. And when a financial crisis struck the United States in 1857, the number of Dutch immigrants dropped significantly. Not until after the Civil War, would it climb again to over a thousand per year.

PART V

From the Civil War to World War I, 1860-1914

1. *The Civil War*

The mainstream of Dutchmen did not go south due to a combination of circumstances. Father VandenBroek, Van Raalte, and Scholte had built their colonies in the northern part of the country. Few immigrants had sufficient capital to establish themselves independently from these settlements. Also, slavery was repugnant to practically every immigrant from The Netherlands.

Like most immigrants, the Dutch settlers tended to join the Democratic party. But they were also strongly opposed to slavery. When the Civil War broke out in 1861, the Dutch loyally met the call for military service in the Union army. Among the many volunteers were Van Raalte's sons. One of them, Dirk B. K. Van Raalte, lost an arm in battle. However, the injury did not prevent him from later becoming politically active as a member of the Michigan state legislature.

Scholte, in Pella, Iowa, at first opposed abolition of slavery on Biblical grounds but later changed his interpretation, and strongly supported President Abraham Lincoln. The Iowa Republicans appointed Scholte to be one of their representatives at the Chicago Convention in 1860. Lincoln and Scholte often exchanged letters. A cane that was a present from Lincoln is still preserved in the Scholte House at Pella.

2. *Integration into American Life*

American citizens of Dutch extraction became increasingly active in politics. This participation in the nation's affairs made the Dutch immigrants into valuable citizens. However, as a group, the Dutch settlers lacked the numerical strength to play a significant role on the state or national level.

Dirk B. K. Van Raalte (born in 1844). He served as a soldier in the Union Army and as a congressman in the Michigan state legislature.

If the original Dutch settlers in New York and New Jersey had organized as a separate body, the influx of new immigrants from The Netherlands might have strengthened them. But Dutchmen arrived at only a fraction of the number of the Germans, Irish, or Italians. No strong and unified Dutch organization made an effort to manipulate the Dutch migration to its advantage. Even the churches' activities among them were not aimed at increasing ethnic strength.

The Catholic Church had to cope with arrivals of widely different nationalities, among whom the Dutch constituted a small minority. To maintain unity, the Catholic Church had to encourage the Americanization of all its immigrant members. American citizenship was therefore stressed more than loyalty to Dutch characteristics.

The Dutch Reformed Church found itself in a similar situation. When the Hudson Valley was still Dutch, the Church's ties with The Netherlands had been very strong. But under British rule it refused to become an active vehicle of anti-British sentiment. Nor did The Netherlands try to encourage this Dutch element to resist England's rule in the area. Opponents left the colony. In the Revolutionary War the several thousand Dutchmen who chose to be Empire Loyalists eventually resettled in Canada. But the Patriots accepted American citizenship, of course. The Dutch Reformed Church, while not entirely forgetting the Loyalists, cast its lot with the new Republic and made itself increasingly independent from supervision in The Netherlands. It gained complete independence by 1790. Although the Church never lost its interest in The Netherlands, it wanted to be an American church and not a Dutch dependency. Thus Catholics and Protestants alike aided in the Americanization of the Dutch immigrants.

3. *Increased Immigration*

After the Civil War ended in 1865, increasing numbers of Dutchmen came to the United States. This increase in Dutch immigration was mainly caused by the rapidly expanding population in The Netherlands. Even though over 200,000 acres of wasteland had been reclaimed from the sea for agriculture, and industry had expanded, The Netherlands was such a small country that its swelling population was difficult to absorb.

After the Civil War, the growing industries in America's Northern states required ever-increasing numbers of workers. At the same time, the Western states still offered to sell cheap land to prospective farmers who wanted to cash in on the rising world demand for grains. Therefore, of the thousands of Dutchmen leaving The Netherlands, many came to North America. Enthusiastic settlers in Michigan, Wisconsin, and Iowa were writing glowing accounts of American prosperity to their relatives in The Netherlands. There Dutch farmers were faced with falling grain prices at a time when massive crops in the United States could be produced at lower costs.

Furthermore, the United States government placed prohibitive tariffs upon foreign imports to protect domestic industries. These tariffs severely penalized several Dutch industries, especially the cigar makers, the diamond workers, and the bulb growers. Many of them were unwilling to give up their trade and decided to leave The Netherlands and reestablish themselves in America.

The increased use of the steam engine facilitated emigration by making transportation across the ocean cheaper.

Workers stream from a New England factory of the 1860's. Industry supplied jobs for many of the immigrants.

In addition, railroad companies in America were competing for passengers. A one-way ticket between New York and Chicago cost no more than five dollars and at one time it was even possible to travel from New York to St. Louis for only a dollar.

All of these factors contributed to a great increase in the number of Dutchmen coming to the United States. Averaging a thousand per year in the period from 1865 to 1880, immigrants began arriving much faster after 1880. This was the period when the greatest number of Dutch immigrants came to America, as shown in the following table.

1880	3,340
1881	8,597
1882	9,517
1883	5,249
1884	4,198
1885	2,689

4. *New Settlements*

Many of these new immigrants settled in the established Dutch colonies. Their presence increased the demand for land, which forced prices up. Several land companies and land-holding railroad firms tried to capitalize on that situation. The land they had previously acquired at very low cost, they sold for less money per acre than land cost in the growing Dutch settlements. The St. Paul and Pacific Railway, for instance, tried to attract Dutchmen to Minnesota by promising to pay half the cost of a new church as soon as 20 Dutch families settled in a designated area.

Frequently, the Dutch settlers — including newcomers and members of the second and third generation — joined together to establish new settlements. For instance, Pella, Iowa, had been such a successful settlement that in 1868 the price of land had climbed to $60 per acre. But equally good land was available at only $1.25 per acre in the unsettled areas north of Sioux City, Iowa.

The number of Dutch settlements increased in regions where land could be bought at low prices with low down payments. Typical examples are Holland, Nebraska (1868), and New Orange, South Dakota (1885). Clergymen often played a decisive role in establishing new settlements.

The committee who chose to settle Sioux County, Iowa. The original settlers were a branch of those who had come to Pella, Iowa.

In Holland, Michigan, the aging Van Raalte resigned from his pulpit in 1867. Concerned as always about the poorer immigrants, he became involved in a prospective settlement in Virginia. He encouraged a group of 200 immigrants to come from The Netherlands to Amelia County where the land was owned by a Dutch real estate agent from New York. Against his advice, the settlers bought more land than they could hope to cultivate. A crop failure in 1870 brought financial ruin to almost everyone. Van Raalte's health was broken, and he returned to Michigan. Although attempts were made to continue the Virginia settlement, the situation became so desperate that in 1876 the remaining settlers moved to Holland, Nebraska.

5. *California*

Several Dutchmen recommended settlement in California. As early as 1871, R.P.A. Dozy claimed that California would ultimately become the most prosperous state. But the Dutch-American Agriculture and Emigration Company, established in The Netherlands to bring Dutch settlers directly to California, failed to attract the necessary capital. This may have been caused by the financial panic of 1873. Even James de Fremery, first Dutch consul in San Francisco, was unable to ignore the crisis. As founder and president of the San Francisco Savings Union, he had agreed to back the Dutch-American Agriculture and Emigration Company but now he could not keep his promise.

James de Fremery founded the San Francisco Savings Union and served as its president from 1862 to 1883. (Courtesy, the Wells Fargo Bank History Room, California)

One "Dutch" settlement that succeeded was populated not by settlers from The Netherlands but by Japanese. It started as a commercial venture directed by the Dutch reclamation engineer P.J. Van Löben Fels, who in 1877 successfully drained the waters from the Sacramento River Delta, east of Sacramento. He called the *polder* (newly reclaimed land protected by dikes), *Vorden* after his native village in the Dutch province of Gelderland. No particular effort was made to attract Dutch settlers, so Japanese gardeners soon worked the polder.

It was not until after World War I that a few Dutch settlements began in California. Dutch-Americans from other states were responsible for the groups of Netherlanders in Redlands, Bellflower, Compton, and other towns. In recent years these communities have received relatively large numbers of new Dutch immigrants.

6. *Church Leadership*

In 1907 the Catholics established the Belgian-Dutch Catholic League of Priests, with headquarters in Chicago, which was supplanted in 1911 by the Catholic Colonization Society of the U.S.A. Its aim was similar to VandenBroek's: to prevent the dispersal of Dutch-speaking Catholic families who might lose contact with the Church and thus lose the faith. The Society's method of operation would be to guarantee land companies that the Society would bring in dependable Catholic settlers in return for a company's financial support of a priest in the new settlement. For example, in 1911 the Society established the town of Butler, in Otter Tail County, Minnesota. Protestants in the area welcomed the Dutch newcomers by donating a bell for their new church. The Society aided the Dutch immigrant both in integrating well into American life and preserving the Catholic faith.

The Dutch Reformed Church willingly aided the Dutch immigrants but did not try to steer the newcomers in definite directions. Especially in the late 1840's, Dutch pastors would arrive in the New World with their entire congregation. After the Civil War most Dutch immigrants arrived individually. The Church simply tried to serve all comers.

Neither Scholte in Pella nor Van Raalte in Holland were able to avoid ecclesiastical problems. Scholte tended to govern his church arbitrarily and according to his version of the truth. This placed him outside the Reformed Church. His very active participation in national politics further complicated the issue. Only a small portion of the Pella settlers remained loyal to Scholte.

Van Raalte faced quite another problem in Michigan. He had been kindly received and aided by the Dutch Reformed Church, especially through its New York pastors DeWitt and Wyckoff. However, Van Raalte was even more impressed by the agreement in doctrinal standards. As a good Calvinist, he wanted to remain within the true church and, hence, to join with the Americanized Reformed Church.

A small but vocal minority resisted this type of Americanization. They wanted to be identified as Dutch in religious as well as cultural matters. In 1857 they seceded from Van Raalte and the Reformed Church. At first they called themselves the True Holland Reformed Church which was later changed to Christian Reformed Church. Fiercely competitive, the two denominations tried to outdo each other in attracting Dutch immigrants.

The Christian Reformed Church grew rapidly in the early 1880's when the Dutch Reformed Church refused to condemn Freemasonry as a sinful movement which church members were not permitted to join. Those dissatisfied with this ruling switched to the Christian Reformed Church.

An 1890 view of Hope College. It was founded at Holland, Michigan, in 1851.

7. *Colleges*

In Holland, Michigan, Van Raalte's Reformed Church founded and developed Hope College and Western Theological Seminary. Van Raalte began his campaign for these schools very early. He almost blackmailed his congregation into supporting this educational venture by threatening to accept a call to another church. The poor settlers had to scrape the money together. Without the generous aid from the Eastern part of the Reformed Church, Van Raalte's educational plans would probably have failed. As it was, the schools have prospered.

In Grand Rapids, Michigan, the Christian Reformed Church established Calvin College and Seminary. Its founders wanted the school to keep in close contact with the Dutch tradition. Americanization was inevitable, of course, and occurred increasingly after the First World War.

Several academies were established, bridging the gap between grade school and college. Some of them, like Northwestern College in Orange City, Iowa, grew into four-year colleges. The schools undoubtedly speeded up the Americanization process. At the same time, they prolonged the split among the Dutch-American Protestants.

8. *Foreign Affairs*

Many immigrants lacked the time to pay much attention to foreign affairs. However, among the Dutch, two notable exceptions occurred.

When the Spanish-American War broke out in 1898, the support of the American Dutch was enthusiastic. They remembered Dutch history and the Eighty Year War with Spain (1568-1648). They thought of the present conflict in earlier terms, as a defense of their freedom against Spanish oppression.

The Boer War in South Africa brought even more excitement. From Holland, Michigan, the Dutch cabled Queen Victoria of England "to turn from war." Mass meetings were held as soon as the first acts of war had been committed. Collections were organized to aid the *Boeren*, the Dutch farmers, against English aggression. The war stirred up nationalistic sentiment. It also strengthened the desire for freedom for all people. For instance, in Grand Rapids, Michigan, Germans and Poles joined the Dutch in a massive demonstration for the *Boeren*. All participants cheered the Poles who pleaded for Polish freedom.

Zwemer Hall at Northwestern College, Orange City, Iowa. The Hall, which was the original classroom building, is still used as a center of administrative work and for classroom instruction. The college was founded in 1882.

PART VI

The World Wars and Beyond

1. *World War I*

Dutch neutrality in World War I (1914-1918) made it easier for Americans of Dutch extraction to support America's position in the war. The many Dutch-Americans who served in the United States armed forces did not have to fight the descendants of their common Dutch ancestors. Their wartime experiences, shared with Americans of multi-racial and multi-national backgrounds, also tended to speed up the process of Americanization.

The war—and fear—sometimes aroused excessive patriotism. It was during the war that the government of the State of Iowa publicly informed foreign language churches that the state could not protect them unless their congregation was given an English translation of the sermon. The well-meant warning did more harm than good. The almost exclusively Dutch-speaking Christian Reformed churches in Iowa were put under enormous pressure, especially since many of them operated parochial schools that taught Dutch. Violent mobs began to attack the churches. In Sully, a church and its parochial school buildings were burned down. Many Dutch-speaking congregations reluctantly began to adopt the English language. If there had been large numbers of new Dutch immigrants, the change to English could perhaps have been challenged. But the war had brought immigration to a standstill. Besides, preference for the Dutch language among old-timers and the second generation did not stem from disloyalty to America, but from a desire to remain as orthodox as possible.

2. *Postwar Immigration*

Cheap land was no longer available after 1890. Thus, the United States Government received pressure to restrict the number of immigrants permitted to enter the country. In 1921 a quota system was introduced that allowed 3,607 Dutch immigrants to enter every year.

Dutch immigrants at Ellis Island, early twentieth century. Each family numbers 13.

In 1924 the quota was reduced to 1,624, but the 1929 revision increased the rate again to 3,153. Dutch migration to the United States was then bound to remain small.

The severe economic crisis (Great Depression) of 1929, which extended well into the thirties, caused a drastic drop in immigration. From 1929 until 1947, a period which includes the Second World War, the yearly quota of 3,153 was never filled. Thus, the Dutch element in the United States could successfully continue its Americanization.

3. *World War II and Beyond*

World War II broke out in 1939. Within a year, Germany attacked and occupied The Netherlands. But Nazi propaganda among the Dutch in The Netherlands as well as in America failed miserably. The Dutch-Americans loyally supported the democratic cause defended by the Allies. The Dutch government (in exile in London) declared war on Japan a few hours after the attack on Pearl Harbor. This declaration preceded even that of the United States.

The alliance formed during the war continued after 1945. The postwar European Recovery Program, popularly known as the Marshall Plan, brought more than one billion dollars in American aid to The Netherlands, close to $100 per Dutchman. This enabled the Dutch to rebuild their devastated country.

In addition, Americans privately shipped tons of food and clothing to relatives and friends abroad. The churches were massively involved in physical and spiritual aid. All nationalities, including the Dutch, participated in these aid programs. They did so over and above the extra taxes required of them for the Marshall Plan.

The results were spectacular. In 1954 The Netherlands was the first country in Europe that no longer wanted Marshall aid. An impressive sign of American-Dutch friendship occurred on September 11, 1959, when Crown Princess Beatrix of The Netherlands landed in New York City for a visit to the United States. Exactly 350 years earlier Henry Hudson had arrived on the *Halve Maen.* The festivities honored the early Dutch settlers. They also underlined continuing good relations not only between The Netherlands and America, but also between the Dutch and the descendants of all the nationalities who constitute the American people.

Bell presented to the United States by the Province of Zeeland in The Netherlands. It was one of 49 carillon bells that The Netherlands offered to America in gratitude for aid given during and after World War II. On May 5, 1960, the carillon bell tower was dedicated in Washington, D.C.

Ice skating was introduced into American life by the Dutch in New Amsterdam. In The Netherlands, skating was a means of travel as well as a form of recreation.

PART VII

Dutch Contributions to American Life and Culture

Since the arrival of the first permanent Dutch settlers in 1624, the Dutch immigrants and their descendants have influenced every aspect of American life. Although the Dutch are only a small percentage of the American population, they have contributed many outstanding individuals, educational institutions, and even words from their language to American life and culture.

1. *Language*

There are many Dutch words that have been part of the English language in America for so long that they have lost some of their original sound and spelling. One of the best known of these words is "boss," which comes from the Dutch *baas* or master. The seafaring Dutch contributed words such as "yacht" *(jacht),* and "skipper" *(schipper).* In the case of the popular Dutch sports of *kolf* (golf) and *schaats* (skating), the activity as well as the name have been part of American life since they were introduced in New Amsterdam by the early Dutch settlers.

Even the rivalry between the early Dutch and English settlers in New Netherland led to common expressions that are still in use. The Dutch referred to New Englanders by the derogatory term of "Yankee" (*Janke*), meaning "Little Johnnies." On the other hand, England's hostility toward The Netherlands in the seventeenth century is reflected in such expressions as: Dutch courage, Dutch comfort, Dutch treat, Dutch uncle, to be in Dutch, and so on. Although these expressions originated in England they were also used in America.

View of Queens, 1862. Rutgers College was chartered in 1766 as Queen's College and opened in 1771 in a New Brunswick tavern. It was not until 1809 that work on the oldest college structure, Queens, was begun. In 1825, the name of the college was changed to honor **Colonel Henry Rutgers,** a significant benefactor.

2. *Higher Education*

The earliest Dutch settlers in New Netherland were less concerned about higher education than those who came in the nineteenth century. The early traders were not interested in permanency. But those who made New Netherland their home grew increasingly concerned about higher learning. Thus the Dutch Reformed Church was instrumental in establishing Queen's College, now Rutgers University at New Brunswick, New Jersey. Although the state of New Jersey assumed control of the University, the Church continues to operate the Theological Seminary at New Brunswick.

Rutgers baseball team, 1890.

Albertus Van Raalte, who had been so intensely engaged in training ministers in The Netherlands, was especially interested in education. Within a few years after arriving in America, Van Raalte forced his settlement at Holland, Michigan, to support a college which he referred to as his "anchor of hope for the future of these people." Aided by the Dutch Reformed Church, both Hope College (1851) and later Western Theological Seminary embarked upon a distinguished course in education. Today, their relations with The Netherlands are cordial but incidental. The schools are completely Americanized. Other institutions of the Dutch Reformed Church are Central College at Pella, Iowa, and Northwestern College at Orange City, Iowa.

Dutch origins lingered longer at Calvin College and Seminary (1876) in Grand Rapids, Michigan. This school serves the Christian Reformed Church and has a separate department for the Dutch language and culture. However, it is in no way a Dutch outpost. The Christian Reformed Church is also the major sponsor of Dordt College in Sioux Center, Iowa, and of Trinity College in Chicago, Illinois.

Through the efforts of the Dutch-Americans and the *Algemeen Nederlands Verbond,* Columbia University established the Queen Wilhelmina Chair in Dutch Culture. A lectureship in Dutch culture was also established at Harvard University in 1967.

Hendrik van Loon (1882-1944) and **Mark Van Doren** (1894-1972). Van Loon wrote and illustrated many children's books. He also wrote and broadcast material for the United States and The Netherlands during World War II. Van Doren took part in many educational radio and television programs, including a series called "Invitation to Learning."

3. *Letters*

Several prominent Dutch-Americans in the field of literature have been associated with Columbia University. The author and journalist, Hendrik Willem van Loon (1882-1944), occupied the Queen Wilhelmina Chair in Dutch Culture which had been established at Columbia. Born in Rotterdam, van Loon came to the United States in 1903. He was an Associated Press correspondent in Russia during the Russian Revolution of 1905 and in Belgium at the beginning of World War I. He is best known for his popular histories, including *The Story of Mankind, The Story of the Bible*, and *America*. In World War II he aided The Netherlands during the German occupation. For this, he was awarded the Order of the Lion of The Netherlands in 1942.

The Van Doren brothers, Carl and Mark, both served on the faculty of Columbia University, both were on the staff of *The Nation* magazine, and both received Pulitzer Prizes. Together they wrote *American and British Literature since 1890*. The older, Carl Van Doren (1885-1950), was a prolific writer and editor. In addition to being literary editor of *The Nation*, and later of *Century Magazine*, he was managing editor of *The Cambridge History of American Literature* and of *The Living Library*. In 1939 he was awarded a Pulitzer Prize for his biography of Benjamin Franklin. Mark Van Doren (1894-1972) was a poet, critic, biographer, and fiction writer. His *Collected Poems, 1922-1938* won a Pulitzer Prize in 1940. He also helped found the Great Books movement.

Authors **Pearl S. Buck** (1892-1973) and **Peter de Vries**. Mrs. Buck won the Pulitzer Prize in 1931 and the Nobel Prize for Literature in 1938. De Vries, an editor for the *New Yorker* magazine, has written such comic novels as *Tunnel of Love* and *Let Me Count the Ways*. In a recent novel called *Forever Panting*, de Vries tells the story of a modern Dutch-American who cannot escape his strict Dutch Reformed upbringing.

Edward William Bok (1863-1930) arrived in America at the age of six. He was the very successful editor of the *Ladies Home Journal* for 30 years, from 1889 until 1919. His autobiography, *The Americanization of Edward Bok*, was awarded a Pulitzer Prize in 1920. As an active philanthropist, he endowed the Woodrow Wilson professorship of literature at Princeton. He also established the famous "Singing Tower Wild Life Sanctuary" at Lake Wales, Florida, which houses the Bok Tower.

Carl Van Vechten (1880-1964) was an accomplished photographer, music critic, and novelist. Among his critical works is *The Music of Spain*, published in 1918. Van Vechten was especially interested in blues music and in promoting better relations between Negroes and whites.

Paul de Kruif (1890-1971) was born in the Dutch-American community of Zeeland, Michigan. After graduating from the University of Michigan, he worked there as a bacteriologist from 1912 to 1917. He soon turned to writing about scientific and medical subjects, especially background facts about medical scientists at work. Some of his books are *Microbe Hunters, The Fight for Life*, and *Hunger Fighters*. He supplied much of the scientific material for Sinclair Lewis's novel *Arrowsmith*.

Although Pearl Sydenstricker Buck (1892-1973) was born in West Virginia, she spent most of her life until 1934 in China and the Far East. Her parents and her first husband, John Lossing Buck, were missionaries there. Her sensitive writings have accurately described the customs and problems of the oriental people and have contributed much to racial understanding. Her second, and perhaps most famous novel, *The Good Earth,* won a Pulitzer Prize in 1931. In 1938, she won the Nobel Prize for Literature, the first American woman to be so honored. Her other novels include *Eastwind: West Wind* (her first book), *The Patriot, Dragon Seed,* and *Letter from Peking.* She also wrote children's books and plays and was active in work for retarded children. In 1949, she founded Welcome House Inc., an adoption agency for children of mixed Asian-American blood.

James Muilenburg (1896-1974) was born in Orange City, Iowa, about 20 years after his grandfather and grandmother with their children had come from The Netherlands by way of New Orleans. With degrees from Northwestern Classical Academy at Orange City, Hope College at Holland, Michigan, the University of Nebraska, and Yale University,

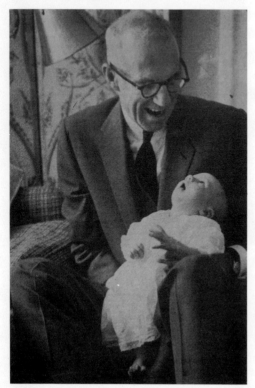

In 1946, **Dr. Benjamin Spock** began his career as a pediatrician and published *The Common Sense Book of Baby and Child Care.* The book, which has sold over 21 million copies, is the best-selling original title published in the United States. In 1968, Dr. Spock was sentenced to two years in prison for conspiring to council boys on how to avoid the draft. As early as 1962 he had stated, "There's no point in raising children if they're going to be burned alive."

Martin Van Buren (1782-1862) was the eighth president of the United States.

Dr. Muilenburg became a renowned professor of the Old Testament and an Orientalist, who taught widely. He was one of the seven translators responsible for the Revised Standard Version of the Old Testament.

4. Government and Politics

Three American Presidents have been of Dutch descent: Martin Van Buren, Theodore Roosevelt, and his distant cousin, Franklin Delano Roosevelt.

Martin Van Buren (1782-1862), eighth President of the United States, was born in the small Dutch community of Kinderhook, New York. He became prominent in the State Democratic party when he served in the New York Senate. Later, he organized his own closely knit political machine called the Albany Regency and served in the United States Senate. He was probably the most influential advisor to President Andrew Jackson, under whom he served as Secretary of State and later as Vice-President. With Jackson's support, Van Buren became President in 1836, and took office shortly before the country's first great financial crisis, the Panic of 1837. The hard times that followed made Van Buren an unpopular President and earned him the nickname of "Van Ruin." He was nominated for President again in 1848 by the anti-slavery Free Soil Party but was defeated. He retired to his birthplace but remained active as a loyal Democrat until his death.

Both Roosevelts were descendants of Klaes Martenszen Van Rosenvelt (later changed to Roosevelt), a Dutch landowner who came to New York from the province of Zeeland in the 1640's. Most of the Van Roosevelts became wealthy landowners and businessmen.

President **Theodore Roosevelt** (1858-1919) organized a volunteer regiment of "Rough Riders" during the Spanish-American War. He was a noted hunter, explorer, and author of books, as well as a politician.

Theodore Roosevelt (1858-1919) was the 26th President of the United States. His political career began as a Republican member of the New York State Legislature. He then served as a reform-minded head of the New York City Police Board, as a member of the U.S. Civil Service Commission, and as Governor of New York. Later, he was Assistant Secretary of the Navy and Vice-President, both under President McKinley, whose assassination in 1901 made "Teddy" Roosevelt President at the age of 42. He was re-elected in 1904. In 1912, he ran for the presidency again on the "Bull Moose" or Progressive Party ticket, but came in second in the three-way race. Roosevelt was the first American to win the Nobel Peace prize (1906) for organizing the peace talks that ended the Russo-Japanese War.

Franklin Delano Roosevelt (1882-1945) became the 32nd President of the United States, after serving as a Democratic member of the New York State Senate, Assistant Secretary of the Navy under Woodrow Wilson, and Governor of New York. He served as President from 1932 until 1945, the only President to be elected to four terms, although he died shortly after his last re-election. Roosevelt's term of office covered the years of America's greatest depression — which precipitated his "New Deal" reform program — and World War II.

Eleanor Roosevelt (1884-1962) was the wife of Franklin and the niece of Theodore Roosevelt. She was a leader in women's organizations and worked for such causes as minority rights, better housing and employment, and consumer welfare. In 1946 she was made chairman of the Commission on Human Rights and from 1945 to 1953

President **Franklin D. Roosevelt** (1882-1945) and his wife, **Eleanor** (1884-1962). Mrs. Roosevelt served as a link between her husband and the world of politics after he became ill with polio. In 1933, she held the first press conference ever given by a President's wife.

(and again in 1961) she was named a United States delegate to the United Nations.

Arthur Hendrik Vandenberg (1884-1951) was an influential Republican senator from Michigan who became one of the leading advocates of a United States bipartisan foreign policy. He served as a delegate to the United Nations and as chairman of the Senate Committee on Foreign Affairs (1948), where he helped direct passage of the European Recovery Program.

John Vliet Lindsay was mayor of New York City from 1965 to 1973, after serving three terms as congressman from New York. He was the first Republican to become mayor of New York City in 20 years. Lindsay's liberal viewpoint and his untiring devotion to the people of New York made him one of the foremost authorities on urban problems.

Arthur Vandenberg (1884-1951), Senator from Michigan.

John Vliet Lindsay, former mayor of New York.

In his youth, millionaire **Cornelius Vander-bilt** ran a freight and passenger ferry be-tween Staten and Manhattan Islands. He later secured the majority of ferry lines and other short lines in the New York City area.

5. Business and Philanthropy

Cornelius Vanderbilt (1794-1877) founded the Vanderbilt family fortune with the $100 million he made in both shipping lines and railroads. "The Commodore," as he was called, started steamship lines to Europe and a line to San Francisco, including an overland route through Nicaragua. At the age of 70, he switched his interest to railroads and became president of the New York Central. He gave one million dollars to found Vanderbilt University in Nashville, Tennessee.

6. The Armed Services

General Alexander A. Vandegrift (1887-1973) was born in Virginia, became a second lieutenant in the United States Marine Corps in 1909, and served as Marine Corps commandant from 1944 to 1947. He was the first Marine Corps officer to hold the rank of permanent general. He retired in 1949.

General James A. Van Fleet, a graduate of the U.S. Military Academy in 1915, saw active service in World Wars I and II and the Korean War. He retired in 1953 but was recalled to active duty in 1961 to help train army guerilla fighters.

Marine **General**
Alexander A. Vandegrift (1887-1973).

Air Force **General**
Hoyt S. Vandenberg (1899-1954).

General Hoyt S. Vandenberg (1899-1954), also a graduate of the U.S. Military Academy, served as an Air Force commander and a chief of staff during World War II. From 1948 until 1953, he was chief of staff of the United States Air Force.

Robert J. Van de Graaff (1901-1966) built the first electrostatic generator. This device (left) aids in atom smashing because it builds up a high electrical charge and generates a constant supply of voltage.

Scientists **William J. Kolff** (left) and **James Van Allen.** It is believed that the charged particles in the Van Allen Radiation Belt originated from giant solar flares that became trapped by the earth's magnetic field.

7. *Science*

Robert J. Van de Graaff (1901-1966) was a physicist and associate professor at the Massachusetts Institute of Technology, where he built the first electrostatic generator (called the "Van de Graaff generator"), an accelerating device used in nuclear research.

Dirk Brouwer (1902-1966) was a Netherlands-born professor of astronomy and director of the observatory at Yale University. From 1941 to 1966, he was also the editor of the *Astronomical Journal.*

Dr. William J. Kolff is a medical doctor who developed the artificial kidney in The Netherlands. After World War II he came to America, where he is working on a comprehensive program of artificial organs at the University of Utah.

Carl L. Norden (1880-1965) came to America from The Netherlands in 1904. He worked in Brooklyn as a mechanical engineer before setting up his own company to design advanced instruments and devices for the Navy. He is most famous as the inventor of the Norden bombsight, a system for automatically pinpointing a ground target from a bombing plane.

Dr. James Van Allen, a physicist, is head of the department of physics and astronomy at the University of Iowa. In 1958, he discovered the Van Allen Radiation Belt, a ring of fast moving, electrically charged particles that surrounds the earth and may someday be a hazard to space travel.

Artist **Willem de Kooning.**

8. *The Arts*

Willem de Kooning was born in Rotterdam in 1904. He came to America in 1926 and became one of the leading abstract expressionist painters of the 1940's. His paintings are characterized by bold outlines and areas of textured color. "Woman I," from a series painted in the 1950's, was one of the most controversial paintings of the decade.

Piet Mondrian (1872-1944) was a Dutch artist known for the geometric, nonobjective style which he called "neoplasticism." He was educated in Amsterdam, and lived in Paris, where the cubist works of Braque and Picasso influenced him. Mondrian, in turn, influenced later architecture and advertising design. Shortly after the beginning of World War II, in 1940, Mondrian came to New York City, where he continued his work until his death.

Frank Van der Stucken (1858-1929) was born in Texas and became conductor of the Cincinnati Symphony Orchestra (1895-1907) and director of the Cincinnati College of Music (1897-1901). He was the first conductor to present an entire concert program of American compositions in the United States and abroad.

Richard Hageman (1882-1966) was the Netherlands-born conductor of the Amsterdam Royal Orchestra, the New York Metropolitan Opera Company, and other orchestras. Among his compositions are *The Crucible,* and *Caponsacchi* (an opera), as well as many film scores.

Conductors **Frank Van der Stucken** (1858-1929) and **Richard Hageman** (1882-1966).

Cecil B. De Mille (1881-1959), an American motion-picture director and producer, was noted for his film "spectacles" using vast, elaborate sets and mass crowd scenes. He was also known as a film-making pioneer. In 1913 he collaborated with Samuel Goldwyn to make the first feature length film in Hollywood, *The Squaw Man.* Two of his most successful movies were *The Greatest Show on Earth* (winner of an Academy Award in 1953) and *The Ten Commandments.*

Agnes De Mille, the niece of Cecil B. De Mille, is an American dancer and choreographer. In 1928, at the age of 20, she made her American concert debut. Later, she created the first important American ballet, *Rodeo,* and was the first to bring the ballet form to musical comedy in the New York stage production of *Oklahoma!* (1943). She also choreographed *Carousel, Brigadoon,* and *Paint Your Wagon.*

Cecil B. De Mille was the first director to use the megaphone and later, the loudspeaker in his work.

Johnny VanderMeer pitched for the Cincinnati Reds from 1936 to 1949, for Chicago in 1950, and for Cleveland in 1951.

Norm Van Brocklin coached the Minnesota Vikings from 1961 to 1967. He coached the Atlanta Falcons from 1968 to 1973.

Jim Kaat, former pitcher for the Minnesota Twins, was sold to the Chicago White Sox in 1973. He now plays for the Philadelphia Phillies.

Diane de Leeuw, winner of the silver medal in women's figure skating at the 1976 Winter Olympics in Innsbruck, Austria. Diane, a citizen of both the United States and The Netherlands, skates for The Netherlands in national competition.

Conclusion

These and other contributions of the Dutch in America bear witness to their successful integration into American life. Because of the rapid Americanization of the Dutch immigrants, all areas of American life opened up to them and their children, enabling them to produce good citizens and prominent people in many fields.

"De Zwaan," a 200-year-old windmill, was imported from The Netherlands in 1965 and restored at Windmill Island Municipal Park in Holland, Michigan. During the Christmas holiday season, lights illumine the 80-foot steel wings of the windmill. It pays tribute to the Dutch heritage so prominent in western Michigan.

...INDEX...

ABOUT THE AUTHOR...

DR. GERRIT J. TENZYTHOFF was born and raised in The Netherlands, where he graduated from the University of Utrecht. During World
War II, he was a prisoner of the Nazis in Germany, but made a successful
escape from Berlin to his homeland in 1943. He emigrated to Canada in
1951 to work among other Dutch immigrants and earned his master's
degree in sacred theology at Union College, University of British Columbia. In 1959, he came to the United States, where he received his M.A.
and Ph.D. degrees in history at the University of Chicago. His doctoral
thesis was entitled: "The Netherlands Reformed Church: Stepmother
of Michigan Pioneer, Albertus C. Van Raalte." The thesis was a detailed
account of the church conflict (1834) in The Netherlands which led to
Dutch emigration in the 1840's.

Dr. tenZythoff has taught at Western Theological Seminary in Holland, Michigan, and at Ohio State University, and he is currently head of
the Religious Studies Department at Southwest Missouri State College.

The IN AMERICA *Series*

We specialize in publishing quality books for
young people. For a complete list please write:

LERNER PUBLICATIONS COMPANY
241 First Avenue North, Minneapolis, Minnesota 55401